RISE ABOVE THE NOISE

How to Stand Out at the Marketing Interview

LEWIS C. LIN

Praise for RISE ABOVE THE NOISE

"For aspiring marketers, Lewis Lin's *Rise Above the Noise* provides a solid grounding, with concrete examples and exercises, on how to stand out during a marketing interview and land that job of your dreams."

— Luanne Calvert, Chief Marketing Officer, VIRGIN AMERICA

"There's so much confusion on how to succeed at the marketing interview, especially challenging case questions. *Rise Above the Noise* examines the most common and challenging interview questions including developing marketing plans, launching new products and dealing with private label competition."

— Philipp von Holtzendorff-Fehling, Chief Marketing Officer, AMERICAN HOME SHIELD, SERVICEMASTER and Former Vice President Marketing, T-MOBILE USA

"Lewis Lin presents both classic and new marketing cases – along with right and wrong approaches – to sharpen your interview impact. Useful for new graduates and mid-career professionals, *Rise Above the Noise* contains marketing analogs and role plays to help you elevate yourself above other candidates."

—Dan Frechtling, Vice President Global Website Products, HIBU PLC and Former Vice President, MATTEL

"I have interviewed countless candidates for marketing roles, and I wish more of them could attack problems this smartly. Follow the step-by-step guidance in this book, and you will set yourself apart from other candidates and succeed in your marketing interviews."

— Scott Shrum, Former Brand Manager, S.C. JOHNSON & SON

"With the intense competition out there for top marketing jobs, *Rise Above the Noise* is a practical yet thorough guide on how you can ace your interview and land the job of your dreams."

- Jason Jennings, Former Senior Marketing Manager, GENERAL MILLS

ALSO BY LEWIS C. LIN

To my wife, a talented marketer, whose keen instincts tell her what makes me happy.

Published by Impact Interview, 677 120th Ave NE, Suite 2A-241, Bellevue, WA 98105.

Several fictitious examples have been used in this book; these examples involve names of real people, places and organizations. Any slights of people, places, or organizations are unintentional.

The author and publisher have made every effort to ensure the accuracy and completeness of information contained in this book. However, we assume no responsibility for errors, inaccuracies, omissions, or any inconsistency herein.

Corporations, organizations and educational institutions: bulk quantity pricing is available. For information, contact lewis@impactinterview.com.

FIRST EDITION / Third Printing

Lin, Lewis C.
Rise Above the Noise: How to Stand Out in the Marketing Interview / Lewis C. Lin.

Table of Contents

CHAPTER 7 DEFENDING AGAINST COMPETITION 132

CHAPTER 8 COMPETING AGAINST PRIVATE LABEL 139

CHAPTER 14 STRATEGIZING: CEO-LEVEL ISSUES 199

CHAPTER 15 ANSWERING OFF-THE-WALL QUESTIONS . 206

CHAPTER 16 ANSWERING BEHAVIORAL INTERVIEW QUESTIONS 211

CHAPTER 17 RISING ABOVE THE NOISE 225

WHAT'S NEXT 228

ACKNOWLEDGMENTS 229

APPENDIX 230

Introduction
It's About the Marketing Interview

You are probably thinking *Rise Above the Noise* is about marketing yourself at the interview. It's not. It's about successfully interviewing for marketing roles.

In this book, I share advice and examples on how to stand out at the marketing interview. If you want to be the top candidate in the marketing interview out of thousands of other interviewees then this book is for you.

I'm not implying that those competing for the roles you want should be dismissed as irrelevant noise. They're not. They're talented marketing professionals.

But as any marketing professional knows, developing a successful marketing campaign is not easy. A lot of companies promote products, and standing out is their goal. Similarly, I want to help you stand out during the marketing interview.

In the book, I've included examples, answers and advice on solving some of the most common and challenging marketing interview questions. For the sake of simplicity, I refer to hypothetical candidates as "he" and hypothetical interviewers as "she."

How to Get the Most Out of this Book

Many of you will appreciate that *Rise Above the Noise* has sample answers to marketing interview questions. You won't find these answers anywhere else. However, don't get tempted into reading the answers as if you were reading a novel!

Instead, when you reach the practice questions I recommend that you:

- Close the book
- Try solving the question(s) on your own
- Compare your response with the sample answer

By doing so, you'll get comfortable answering questions that most candidates find difficult. You'll also absorb the marketing concepts more deeply. And you'll create an efficient feedback learning loop where you'll deduce where your response came up short and where it surpassed the sample answer.

Scorecard

Each one of the sample answers is given a grade: excellent, above average, average, below average or poor. Each response is evaluated along the following dimensions:

Marketing Aptitude

Does the candidate demonstrate mastery of marketing fundamentals? In an excellent response, a candidate's answer appreciates the nuances of marketing strategy and tactics. He also applies strategic and tactical elements appropriately.

In a poor response, the candidate recites canned marketing frameworks without full understanding of why it's important and how it applies to the bigger picture. Also, he utilizes marketing terminology and concepts incorrectly. Lastly, inexperienced candidates are more likely to limit their marketing plan to a single tactic such as social media.

Plan

Does the candidate know how to approach the question? In an excellent response, the candidate shares how he plans to tackle a hypothetical marketing situation. An excellent response focuses on critical issues and ignores trivial ones.

A poor response meanders through the question, asking for irrelevant details. The interviewer's is often confused by the goal, direction and intent of the candidate's response.

Communication Skills

Does the candidate communicate his ideas clearly and succinctly? An excellent response demonstrates impact and answers the who, what, why, when and where.

A poor response struggles to answer what is happening and the context surrounding an issue. The interviewer has to ask repeated follow-up questions to understand the situation and why it's important. If it's a behavioral question, the interviewer may be confused with the candidate's role in the situation.

Composure

Does the candidate demonstrate composure when responding? Would the interviewer feel comfortable having the candidate present to a senior executive or an important client? An excellent candidate will exude confidence and mastery of details. He will also react appropriately to constructive criticism.

A poor candidate will hesitate to answer a question. He will be afraid to take a stand, fearing that he'll say the wrong thing. If an interviewer reacts to his response with a critical comment, he is unsure of how to respond. He may even get defensive when facing criticism.

Satisfying Conclusion

An excellent response has a satisfying conclusion. The response makes sense, and there are no lingering doubts. If a clear opinion is required, the candidate states it. If the candidate is asked to make a recommendation, the interviewer is clear on what the next steps should be.

A poor response leaves the interviewer in a cloud of confusion. The interviewer is not clear what was being communicated or what the intent is. The candidate may have failed to make a clear stance or conclusion.

Overall Rating

Each response is also given an overall rating. You can think of it as a combination of all the criteria above. The overall rating can also be equated with the overall impression.

One More Thing

Finally, for those of you were hoping for tips on how to market yourself don't worry, I won't disappoint you. I've saved the last chapter for some thoughts on how you can build a unique personal brand that resonates beyond the interview.

Enjoy the book, rise above the noise and get that marketing job offer.

Lewis C. Lin
February 2014

P.S. I'm always interested in hearing from readers. To send a note, ask a question or report typos just email lewis@impactinterview.com.

Chapter 1 The Marketing Interview

To understand the marketing interview, we need to understand the marketing job description. The job description provides clues about what interviewers want in their ideal candidate and the questions they might ask.

Looking at a job description closely puts marketing candidates, both experienced and newcomers, on the same page.

This one comes from Procter & Gamble:

Title

Assistant Brand Manager, Procter & Gamble (P&G)

Mission

P&G Marketing is a global community of the world's best Brand Builders and Business Leaders. We are dedicated to growing Brand and Category share leadership and to empower our succeeding generations to do the same. In short, we are passionate about building Brands that last forever.

Key Responsibilities

Starting as an Assistant Brand Manager in P&G, you will typically develop skills in brand strategy, advertising, PR, consumer bonding, direct-to-consumer marketing and project management. Specifically, you will recommend, develop and execute marketing strategies, plans and programs that build on consumer and customer insights for a consumer brand. You will be responsible for initiatives, projects and day-to-day operations relating to all aspects of the brand business. You will also be using your skills to analyze the consumer, trade and market dynamics as well as the business status, in order to turn them into business plans.

Under the leadership of the Brand Manager, your key responsibilities will include:

- *Developing brand strategies and plans, including strategy, concept and packaging development; product and marketing qualification; and forecasting*
- *Advertising, including strategy and creative brief development; copy evaluation; copy clearance; commercial production and copy testing*
- *Below-the-line consumer communication including print, outdoor, direct-to-consumer marketing, public relations and point of sell materials*
- *Media, including development and execution of media strategies to reach target consumers including level, mix and market prioritization*
- *Manage a multi-functional project team to ensure excellence in execution, including initiative, promotion/pricing plan development, planning, execution and summarizing results*
- *Consumer, customer and market understanding, including detailed business analysis to identify business drivers and opportunities*
- *Complex business and financial analysis*
- *Interpersonal projects, including coaching, training, recruiting, and multi-functional teamwork*

Qualifications

- *Leadership and influencing skills*
- *Strategic thinking and problem solving skills*
- *Ability to work well with others as a team*
- *Innovative and analytical mindset*
- *Ability to adapt to change*

The Ideal Marketing Candidate

This interviewer is looking for candidates with skills or potential in the following areas:

- Marketing strategy
- Advertising
- Media strategies
- Project execution
- Customer insight and research
- Quantitative analysis
- Interpersonal skills

The Marketing Interview

You might be tested with case or behavioral interview questions. Case questions are based on hypothetical business situations and are meant to assess your ability to think on the spot. Behavioral questions are based on your past experience and are popular with hiring managers who believe past performance contributes to future success.

Here's a list of companies that generally do not use case interviews during their marketing interview process. However, please note that this is not a firm rule. The choice to use case, behavioral, or any other interview question types varies from situation to situation. For example, P&G do not ask external candidates case interview questions, but internal candidates are often asked a mixture of hypothetical and case interview questions.

List of Companies that Do Not Use Case Interviews

- Kellogg Company
- Procter & Gamble
- Purina
- SC Johnson

- Starbucks

You may ask the recruiter, hiring manager, or other corporate contact about the questions you could expect. Don't waste time preparing for unlikely questions. At the same time, don't be surprised if an interviewer asks you an oddball question like, "Who's your favorite rapper?" The interviewers are in a position to ask almost anything they wish.

Potential Marketing Interview Question Types

Competency	Question type
Advertising	Questions around critiquing advertising campaigns
Marketing strategy, customer insight and media strategies	Questions about creating marketing plans
Business and quantitative analysis	Pricing, business case and estimation questions
Project execution & interpersonal skills	Behavioral interview questions

Chapter 2 Creating a Positioning Statement

A popular marketing interview question is: "Create a positioning statement for our product."

A positioning statement is usually a sentence that addresses the following:

- What is the product?
- Who is it for?
- Why should I buy it?
- Why is it better than competing alternatives?

Here's an example:

> *Targeted to performance-seeking parents, the Honda Odyssey is a minivan offering plenty of room and amenities for the family, while providing sporty handling and a powerful engine, unlike the Toyota Sienna and the Dodge Grand Caravan.*

Positioning statements play an important part in a marketing organization. Marketers use the positioning statement to guide development of marketing materials, whether it's a brochure or text on a web page. Ideally all marketing materials reinforce the positioning statement's main message.

What is the Interviewer Looking For?

When asking candidates to create a positioning statement, the interviewer is evaluating a candidate's ability to:

- Connect with the customer
- Identify the brand promise (or product benefit) and provide a clear reason to believe the brand promise

- Understand the competition

How to Approach the Question

Answer the question with this positioning statement template in mind.

Positioning Statement Template

For [target end user]

Who wants/needs [compelling reason to buy]

The [product name] is a [product category]

That provides [key benefit].

Unlike [main competitor],

The [product name] [key differentiation]

This widely accepted positioning template was developed by Geoffrey Moore, the author of *Crossing the Chasm*, a book about marketing high-tech products. As with any template or framework, this is meant to be a guideline or checklist. Rigorously applying the template during the interview may sound too formal, boring or academic.

For a more informal approach to positioning statements, consider a product slogan instead. We can see that many brand and product slogans can double as effective positioning statements:

Brand	Slogan	Implied Benefit
Avis	We Try Harder	Customer service
BMW	Ultimate Driving Machine	Thrill & excitement
Miller Light	Great Taste…Less Filling	Low-calorie
Wheaties	Breakfast of Champions	Performance

If you have to develop a position statement for a product, I'd recommend a hybrid of a corporate slogan and the positioning template. You want a slogan's pizzazz and the template's comprehensiveness.

Evaluating Positioning Statements

When evaluating responses to a positioning question, here's what interviewers are looking for in a positioning statement:

- Is it unique and memorable?
- Is it different from that of the competition?
- Will consumers believe it and why will they believe it?
- Can the company use it to create marketing materials?

One and Only One Product Benefit

Don't be tempted to name multiple benefits in a positioning statement. There are several reasons why this isn't ideal.

Ogilvy for Volvo

First, every brand should strive to be the most esteemed company in their category; we call that the brand leader.

Imagine a consumer who wants to buy a car highly rated for safety. Volvo is the brand leader in the safe car category. There could be cars that are safer than Volvo, but it's a strong bet that a safety-minded consumer would at least consider a Volvo. And by being considered, Volvo increases the likelihood that a consumer will purchase.

Second, once brand leadership is attained, it's easy to retain and defend. For over 100 years, Pepsi competed against Coca-Cola. And Pepsi marketers have research studies that prove their product consistently beats Coca-Cola in blind taste tests. Despite Pepsi's efforts to create better tasting products or amp up their marketing efforts, it's unlikely that Pepsi can convince consumers that they are the top cola brand anytime soon.

Can a Brand Claim Leadership in Two Different Categories?

History says no. Countless market leaders have attempted to straddle multiple product benefits, only to have a more focused challenger outcompete them on a single benefit. Here are some examples:

Unfocused market leader	Multiple product benefits	Focused challenger	Single product benefit
Emery Air Freight	Overnight, Two or Three day service, large packages and small packages	FedEx	Overnight
Chevrolet	Large, small, inexpensive, expensive	Mercedes-Benz	Prestige
Tic Tac	Freshen breath, taste, low-calorie, fun, color, sounds	Altoids	Freshen breath

Brands that lead in multiple categories are likely competing with inferior competitors. It's unlikely they would maintain that multiple category brand leadership over the long-term.

To recap, by focusing on a single product benefit, a brand is better positioned to win category leadership. And winning category leadership increases the effectiveness of a brand's marketing efforts and the likelihood of a sale.

Marketers claim multiple product benefits will unlikely gain category leadership and its attendant benefits. Consumers will lose track for what your brand stands for and in the process, forget when and why they should purchase your brand.

Practice Question

1. How would you position the Samsung Chromebook?

Answer

How would you position the Samsung Chromebook?

CANDIDATE: I can't come up with a positioning statement on the spot. Most marketing professionals spend three months to perfect a position statement.

Interviewer gets annoyed with the candidate's attempt to deflect the question

INTERVIEWER: I get your concerns, but I want you to try.

CANDIDATE: Give me a second to collect my thoughts.

Candidate takes 45 seconds

CANDIDATE: Here's my positioning statement: "Targeted at current notebook users, the Samsung Chromebook is a device that competes with the iPad. It can be considered as a tablet with a keyboard at half the price of Apple's tablet. It provides a fast web searching and surfing experience."

INTERVIEWER: I'm not impressed. I have three problems with this:

First, the Chromebook does not compete with the iPad. A Chromebook is a laptop computer that competes with Macs and PCs. Google's product that competes with the iPad is the Android tablet.

Second, I'm pretty sure that most notebook users don't need a second laptop.

Lastly, you don't offer convincing evidence why this product has a "fast web search and surfing experience."

CANDIDATE: Let me give it another shot.

Candidate takes 30 seconds

CANDIDATE: Here's my second attempt: "For users that want an easy-to-use machine at a low price, the Chromebook is the highest quality laptop around. It's the best machine for the Google ecosystem."

INTERVIEWER: This is better than you first attempt, but it's still unsatisfying. I don't know who your target audience is, and you don't define the Google ecosystem. You use several superlatives including "easy-to-use," "highest quality" and "best machine" without evidence.

CANDIDATE: Sorry.

Scorecard

Overall Rating	Poor
Marketing Aptitude	Poor
Plan	Below Average
Communication Skills	Poor
Composure	Poor
Satisfying Conclusion	Excellent

Comments

This is how a below average candidate responds to a positioning statement question. They are reluctant to answer, apply the positioning template incorrectly and respond poorly to interviewer criticism.

Albeit a bit blunt, the interviewer provides detailed insight on why the candidate's two attempts are lacking.

Here's what I would consider as a model response:

> *"For first-time computer buyers, such as students and grandparents, the Samsung Chromebook is as sexy as the MacBook Air but costs 80 percent less."*

It clearly articulates the target audience and lays out the product benefit. It also identifies the competition and why it's different. Finally, the last phrase, "Samsung Chromebook is as sexy as the MacBook Air but costs 80 percent less," has the zest that the interviewer can easily imagine as a smart product tagline.

Chapter 3 Developing Marketing Campaigns

When asked, "You have $1 million dollars. Walk me through your marketing plan for this product" candidates usually freeze with fear. Less-experienced marketers are likely thinking, "I've never had a million dollar marketing budget. How do I know what to do?" Experienced marketers probably think, "I can tell you what to do with it. But I can't tell you now. I need three to six months and a team of people to brainstorm and iterate before executing on a marketing plan."

It's a question that both new and experienced marketers find unreasonable, but there are reasons why interviewers ask it.

What is the Interviewer Looking For?

For a question about developing a marketing campaign, the interviewer is looking for the following:

- *Tactical creativity.* Is the candidate suggesting tactics that are unique and creative? Do they inspire? And are they reasonably effective?
- *Strategic thinking.* Are the suggestions reasonable, logical and relevant to the business objectives?
- *Marketing aptitude.* Does his response cover all the parts, strategic and tactical, with sufficient depth?

Where Most Candidates Make Mistakes

When asked this question, here are the most common mistakes that candidates make on this question. They don't:

1. Clarify objectives.
2. Define who the target customer is.
3. Call out what the positioning message is.

4. Link tactics with objectives or the target customer.

5. Utilize the product positioning when brainstorming objectives.

What usually happens is candidates rattle off a long list of marketing tactics. Without appropriate context, interviewers can be under-whelmed with what they perceive as a random, unrelated list of tactics.

How to Approach the Question

After working with hundreds of clients, I've found that the most effective way to answer interview questions about marketing plans and campaigns is the Big Picture framework.

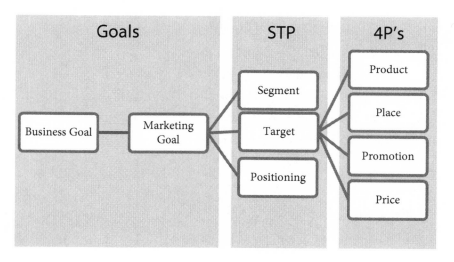

There are three parts to the Big Picture framework: goals, STP (segmentation, targeting and positioning) and the 4P's (product, place, promotion and price.) MBA graduates may recall STP and 4P's from school.

By stating goals, you clarify the purpose of your marketing activity and provide a benchmark on which to measure your marketing plan. Goals focus your time, energy and resources and make it easy to figure out where your priorities should be.

STP is important because customers are too different in their needs. A company cannot serve all customers well. A company needs to pick a segment that they can satisfy thoroughly. And the corresponding customer segment needs to believe that the company understands their problems and has the right solution.

4P's specifies the tactical marketing plan on how to fulfill customers' needs. It describes the product(s), the price customer pays, where they can buy it as well as how they'll hear about it and try it.

There are several reasons why I like the Big Picture framework:

- *It's comprehensive and complete.* This end-to-end framework includes all the key components of any marketing plan.
- *It covers both strategy and creative skills.* It forces candidates to develop a strategy before brainstorming tactical ideas.
- *It showcases thought leadership.* Few candidates, or even marketing employees, can talk about marketing in such sophisticated, convincing terms.

The Big Picture Framework was developed Christie Nordhielm, a University of Michigan marketing professor. In this book, I've modified her original framework to make it easier to learn and apply at the job interview. When you get a marketing plan or campaign interview question, I'd like you to apply the Big Picture framework. Let's dive in and explore each step.

Goals

There are two types of goals you need to consider in your interview response. The first is the overall business objective. The second is the intermediate marketing objectives that contribute to your overall business objective. We'll discuss each in more detail.

Business Goal

Your marketing plan must have a purpose. Specify a business goal at the beginning of your response. Don't craft a motto, buy a Super Bowl TV ad or order corporate T-shirts without cause.

Here are some potential business goals for your marketing plan:

- Profits
- Revenues
- Market share

Most marketing roles are focused on demand generation. As a result, revenue and market share are the most likely goals for your marketing plan.

Theoretically, we would like marketers to have profit goals. It would align their incentives with what's ultimately important for the enterprise. However, there are many levers that affect overall profitability that are outside of the marketer's control, including cost management and product development.

Specify the timeframe for your targeted goal. Deadlines can affect your plan's scope and range of potential tactics.

Here's an example of a well-stated goal:

- *Increase US market share of sugar-free energy drinks by 300 basis points among men and women between 25 to 34 years of age within the next 12 months.*

Here are some examples of poorly stated goals:

- *To introduce our sugar-free energy drink nationwide.*
- *To create awareness that our energy drink is tasty, but sugar-free.*

- *To reach a young, affluent audience for our energy-drink through a television campaign.*

When comparing the two, we quickly see what differentiates strong vs. weak goals. Strong goals are:

- Specific, not vague.
- Measurable.
- Time-bound.

Conceiving strong goals is hard. It takes effort to think through what to achieve in a marketing plan. Another reason why most marketers avoid goals that are specific, measurable and time-bound: fear of failure. By leaving goals vague, success or failure will be a matter of inconclusive debate.

Don't default to corporate customs. Specify strong goals in your marketing interview.

An Alternative Business Goal: Usage

Usage goals are common for marketers whose companies sell products and services on a recurring basis. Marketers for fitness centers typical focus on usage goals, because membership passes sell on an annual basis.

Fitness centers are more likely to get renewals if members perceive value from their membership, be it by visiting the club often or attending fitness classes. So fitness center marketers try to get members to use the club frequently. Other organizations that sell products on a subscription basis include newspapers, magazines and software companies.

Marketing Goal

In addition to the business goal, it's important to state a marketing goal. An easy way to think of marketing objectives is to think of the marketing funnel. The marketing funnel maps the customer journey toward a purchase.

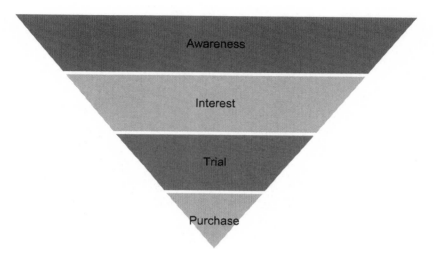

Rise Above the Noise

- *Awareness* is to bring recognition to a product brand.
- *Interest* is to stir fascination with a product: what it does, how it works and what benefit it delivers.
- *Trial* is to compel a prospective user to try the product.
- *Purchase* is, as the name implies, to get a customer to buy into a product.

All products can benefit from increased awareness, interest, trial and purchase. During the interview, to say you want to "do it all" will seem a little too cavalier. Be thoughtful and prioritize for the interviewer.

Which marketing objective will bring about the biggest impact? In general,

- Awareness is most important for new products.

- If awareness is not an issue, focus on interest, especially if products have unknown value propositions or negative reputations.
- If awareness and interest is not an issue, getting the customer to the trial phase should be the goal, especially for products that need to be experienced to appreciate the benefits.
- If awareness, interest and trial are not issues, purchase should be emphasized.

Two additional questions can help us determine our marketing focus:

- Are we looking to acquire new customers or retain existing customers?
- Are we looking to stimulate category demand, or are we looking to steal share from competitors?

Acquisition vs. Retention

Retention

Customer retention is usually more profitable than customer acquisition. Existing customers generate the most revenue because they are:

- More likely to purchase frequently
- More likely to try new and related products
- More likely to refer you to their friends

They are also less costly to service because they are less likely to need:

- An introduction to the category
- Knowledge about the brand
- Information about how the product works
- Customer support
- Discounts or promotions to continue as current customers

Since companies can typically skip the money and effort to educate current customers about the category, brand, or how the products work, companies just need to remind customers of the product benefit.

Acquisition

For some companies, a retention-only strategy is not a choice. Mature companies may be looking for new growth opportunities, so they may try to tap into new customer segments or international markets. Newer companies may not have enough customers to subsist on a retention-only strategy, so they may have to go after new customers, despite the increased cost.

Steal Share or Increase Category Demand

Stealing Share

When evaluating the marketing goal, it's also useful to consider whether a brand should steal share or increase category demand.

Stealing share is acquiring new customers by convincing your competitor's customers to switch to your brand. The advantage of stealing share is that marketers leverage the existing awareness of a brand or category. This saves them from the cost and effort of educating the customer. Instead, a steal share campaign focuses on differentiation from the competition.

Most people think of stealing share as stealing customers from a competitive brand. However, a marketer can also steal customers from a different product category. For example, Red Bull could convince iced coffee drinkers to drink Red Bull instead to stay awake.

A steal share strategy is not normally recommended for market leaders. A market leader's steal share campaign can inadvertently increase awareness of the competitor.

Microsoft recently violated this rule. It hired famous reality TV star, Rick Harrison of Pawn Stars, to attack the Google Chromebook laptop computer, calling it inferior to Windows-based laptops.

This move backfired on Microsoft. It called more attention to the recently launched Google Chromebook, which had limited awareness and interest from consumers, at that time.

Increasing Category Demand

Increasing category demand is about focusing a marketing effort around the category benefit.

Increasing category demand is a natural fit for category leaders. Any incremental demand from these marketing efforts will benefit the market leader more so than smaller players in the category. Consumers, when purchasing in a new category for the first time, are more likely to buy the market leader. New consumers believe the market leader must be best because others who have purchased before them have voted with their wallets.

Increasing category demand also works well for all competitors in new categories, regardless of their market share. In new categories, there are few, if any, competitors. For companies competing in a new category, the biggest challenge is to convince customers to buy from the category. At that stage of a new category's lifecycle, it makes more sense to convince users why they should adopt a new category of products instead of slamming the competition.

There are typically three ways to increase category demand:

1. *Introduce the category to new users.* For example, a company could target new geographic markets.
2. *Convince existing users to buy more.* For example, Brita could encourage customers to replace Brita filters more frequently from once every three months to once a month.
3. *Convince users to use products more frequently.* For example, a smoothie company, Jamba Juice, could sway customers to purchase smoothies not only as refreshment but also as nutrient replenishment after a workout.

STP (Segmentation, Targeting and Positioning)

We group segmentation, targeting and positioning in a single acronym, STP, because all three are part of a logical sequence of strategic marketing choices. With segmentation, we survey all the possible customer groups a company can serve. With targeting, we select a segment that our company can serve best, given our abilities and other competitors in the category. Lastly, the positioning statement communicates to that target segment why they should buy the product. The positioning statement also focuses our decisions when determining marketing tactics.

Segmentation

Segmentation is grouping buyers by attributes. By segmenting the market, it's easier to identify clusters of customers for which the product benefit would resonate most strongly. While marketers would like to sell their product to anyone with a checkbook, most don't have the marketing budget to effectively sell to everyone. Segmentation conserves our resources and concentrates those limited resources on those most likely to purchase.

To segment a customer audience, we create groupings that:

- Have reasonable revenue potential.
- Seek the product benefit.
- Can be accessed through marketing.
- Can be efficiently converted from prospect to purchase.

To help us identify marketing segments that meet the above criteria, let's explore four categories of segmentation: demographic, behavioral, attitudinal and aspirational.

Demographic segmentation groups potential customers based on statistical characteristics of a population. Age, gender, income and occupation are examples of demographic variables.

Behavioral segmentation groups customers based on what they do. For instance, when it comes to clothes-drying behavior, some air dry their clothes. Others use a drying machine.

Attitudinal segmentation groups customers based on what they think. For example, some consumers' believe fast food is convenient. Others believe it is a fun way to eat with the family.

Aspirational segmentation groups customers based on wishes and desires. For example, some consumers may wish to be perceived as well-read. Others want to be viewed as fashionable and trendy.

Demographic segmentation is considered the least sophisticated. Why? Demographic segmentation imperfectly generalizes a brand's customers. For instance, a marketer for Mazda Miata may target a demographic segment of young, urban women between the ages of 25-34. What happens if a 65 year old male wants a fun, inexpensive sports car? Does the Mazda salesman tell him that a Miata isn't meant for him? You can imagine this customer protest by saying, "Not all 65 year old men drive Cadillacs. Let me buy my Miata."

Aspirational segmentation is considered the most sophisticated. Aspirational segments aren't limited by demographic groupings. Instead, they appeal to consumers' dreams and goals. Aspirational segments are also very difficult to obtain. Just imagine, how would a marketer buy a list of customers aspire to be masculine?

The most respected brands typically promote and deliver on aspirational benefits. Some examples:

Brand	Category	Aspirational benefit
Chanel	Leather goods	Luxury
Johnnie Walker	Whiskey	Sophistication
Old Spice	Male grooming	Virility
Versace	Apparel	Fashion

Primary and Secondary Variables

Let's look at segments for two types of variables: primary and secondary.

The primary variable is the category benefit. For instance, in fast food, the category benefit is convenient food.

The secondary variable is a benefit that differentiates a brand from the competition. Here are some secondary variable examples in fast food:

- Wendy's: taste
- Subway: healthy
- Burger King: customization

Perceptual Map

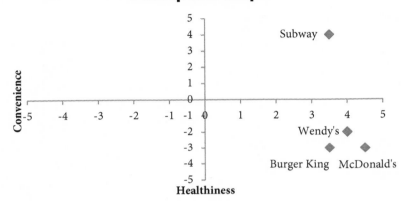

Rise Above the Noise

We can visually portray customer perceptions on a diagram that's called a perceptual map. On the x-axis, we have the primary variable, convenience. On the y-axis, we have the secondary variable, healthiness. We see that Subway astutely chose a secondary variable where they are superior to the competition.

Targeting

Brands should select target segments that appreciate and seek out their brand's product benefit. Subway may seek behavioral segments that eat healthy. It may also seek aspirational segments that wish to be healthy. These consumers are more likely to convert and purchase Subway's sandwiches.

Positioning

The next step is to craft the positioning statement. I discussed the positioning statement in the previous section, so I won't rehash it here.

The 4P's (Product, Place, Promotion and Price)

The 4P's transitions the marketing plan from strategic to tactical elements. Also, known as the marketing mix, the 4P's details the execution plan for the brand offering including:

- What is the product? (Product)
- Where is it sold? (Place)
- And how customers will hear about the product, generate interest and ultimately make a purchase? (Promotion)
- How much does it cost? (Price)

Product

During the marketing interview, you might be asked to improve or invent a product. Use the CIRCLES Method™ below to develop new product ideas. In case you forget, remember that designers love circles. Therefore CIRCLES Method™ is perfect for questions on improving and designing new products.

C omprehend the Situation
I dentify the Customer
R eport the Customer's Needs
C ut, Through Prioritization
L ist Solutions
E valuate Tradeoffs
S ummarize Your Recommendation

As an example, we'll work through the CIRCLES Method™ with Tide Pods:

Comprehend the Situation

For Tide, the company is likely looking for effective ways to steal share from competitors, given the mature detergent market.

Identify the Customer

We can look at customer segments in different ways: demographics, behaviors (washing machine users vs. non-users), attitudes (bleach is only way to keep clothes white) and aspirations ("I want to be known as organized"). For this discussion, we'll go with the washing machine users.

Report the Customer's Needs

Perhaps the top three customer needs, when it comes to washing their laundry, are:

1. Get cleaner clothes.
2. Determine the right amount of detergent.
3. Minimize laundry mess.

Cut, Through Prioritization

We can rule out the first two. Most people are pretty happy with how clean their clothes are. And if you ask the average consumer, measuring detergent is not a problem. But messy laundry rooms are an issue.

List Solutions

The reason it gets messy: consumers are imprecise when measuring dry or liquid detergent. If we eliminated measuring, would that eliminate the mess? How could we eliminate measuring? Drawing inspiration from medicine, capsules have been helpful in minimizing measuring challenges with cough syrup. Should we create a capsule form of detergent? Other ideas could include inventing a washing machine that doesn't require detergent or detergent in a soluble plastic pouch. (For the sake of space, we won't go into details here.)

Evaluate Tradeoffs

The soluble plastic pouch is convenient and easy to transport. However, it's expensive to manufacture and the plastic pouch doesn't dissolve two percent of the time.

Summarize the Recommendation.

Invent pre-measured detergent in a plastic package; the plastic package dissolves during the laundry cycle. The main benefit: eliminate the mess from measuring detergent, while getting clothes clean. The reason this new product is possible now is because Cyberpac, a United Kingdom packaging company, just invented a hydro-degradable plastic in 2009.

Place

When choosing distribution channels, we choose the one that best maximizes revenue. Another way of looking at that is through this formula:

Revenue = (Average Selling Price) * (Number of Units)

There are other things to consider when selecting distribution channels:

- *High involvement products.* Complicated products that require detailed explanation and demonstration are best suited for an in-person — rather than online — retail experience.
- *Steal share strategies.* Brands focused on stealing share would benefit from a retail channel that allows comparison against other products.
- *Acquisition strategies.* Acquisition-focused brands want the broadest reach possible. Such brands should utilize as many distribution channels as they need to get the reach they want.
- *Retention strategies.* Brands focused on retention favor communication channels that allow them to communicate directly with customers without involving an intermediary. This minimizes restrictions on the content and frequency of their communication.

Promotion

As a marketer, you want to choose promotional tactics that match your strategies. For your reference, here's a list of potential marketing tactics:

Consumer Promotions

Item	Example
Brochures	Vespa scooters created a brochure that looked like a well-worn travel journal, inspiring romance and adventure
Direct mail	Online casino, Bodog.com, used a billfold wallet with a $100 to encourage new customers to try their site
Email marketing	STA Travel uses email marketing to promote Cyber Monday deals
Newsletters	Godiva Rewards Club sends a monthly e-newsletter called Godiva Chocolate Notes
Outdoor	BMW and Audi have billboards promoting their new models
Print	Google's Moto X print ad changes colors, demonstrating the phone's customization capabilities
Radio	Heinz used a radio to demonstrate that British breakfasts wouldn't be the same without Heinz ketchup
Telephone	Barack Obama sent text messages to his supporters when he chose his vice presidential nominee in 2008
Television	Apple used a TV ad that appealed to aspirational creative types with its "Think Different" campaign

Trade Promotions

Item	Description	Example
Contests	Offers to win prizes after a purchase	McDonald's Monopoly game gives tokens upon purchase to win cash and prizes
Coupons	Voucher for a price discount on a product	Oral-B provides a $3 coupon for its electric toothbrush
Loyalty Programs	Reward customers for frequent purchases or visits	American Airlines has a program that gives loyal customers "miles" that could be converted into free flights
Premiums	Accompanying merchandise offered to entice customers to purchase another product	Clorox Disinfecting Wipes 5-Pack comes free with a Clorox Bleach Pen
Price Packs	Price reductions that are marked directly on the packaging	Both Pantene shampoo and conditioner are sold together in a shrink-wrapped package from the

		manufacturer
Rebates	Refund on purchase price	A computer purchase comes with a $30 rebate
Samples	Free amount of product, meant to drive a product trial	Colgate mails toothpaste samples to consumers

Other Tactics

Item	Description	Example
Free consultations	Free service establishes relationship and trust	Jiffy Lube provides free brake inspections
Public relations	Sharing information with the public through a variety of channels including press and conferences	Theo's Chocolate made Oprah's best of 2008 list
Referral program	Company process to facilitate word-of-mouth marketing	T-Mobile offers a $25 credit for each friend that a customer signs up to T-Mobile
Seminars or webinars	Training event for marketing purposes, usually held at a conference	Google offers free seminars to demonstrate how small businesses can advertise on the Google search engine
Social media	Building online conversation and communities using social networks such as Facebook, Twitter and YouTube	Cadbury created an edible chocolate thumb, in honor of the one million fans that clicked on the Facebook "Like" thumb on Cadbury's Facebook page
Sponsorships	Gain publicity and audience access by attaching a brand to an event	Red Bull sponsors the X Games, an extreme sports event
Street marketing	Promoting products in a public place	BMW added a Styrofoam replica of a Mini-Cooper to the side of a downtown Houston building
Testimonials	A customer statement praising a product	Subway used Jared Fogel's weight loss story as a testimonial for their healthy sandwiches
Trade shows	Exhibition where	Samsung announced a new

For each media type, you'd want to consider both reach and impact.

- *Reach* is defined as the number people who are exposed to an advertisement. Super Bowl TV ads, considered the paramount of reach, reach an average TV audience of 111 million viewers.

- *Impact* is defined as the value of an exposure. If you're an e-commerce retailer, you're likely to find it more valuable to advertise online as opposed to on a billboard. The reason is a customer is more likely to make an online purchase if they're already at a computer. Conversion rate and average revenue per conversion are metrics commonly used to track a tactic's impact.

Price

We'll cover price later in the book, so we'll skip it for now.

Practice Questions

1. What promotional strategies would you use for a Honey Nut Cheerios campaign?
2. Develop a social good campaign for Teavana.
3. How would you market Google AdWords?
4. How would you market Halos?

Answers

What promotional strategies would you use for a Honey Nut Cheerios campaign?

Screenshot / @ Cheerios

CANDIDATE: This will be fun. I grew up eating Honey Nut Cheerios! To start, I'd like to ask some clarifying questions.

INTERVIEWER: Sure.

CANDIDATE: What is the goal of this new promotional campaign? For instance, are we trying to increase revenue or market share?

INTERVIEWER: Yes, the goal is to increase revenue for the cereal.

CANDIDATE: How much?

INTERVIEWER: Five percent.

CANDIDATE: What timeframe are we looking at?

INTERVIEWER: One year.

CANDIDATE: It's been a while since I watched any commercials for the cereal, so I'm a little out of touch with the target customer. Can you share the current value proposition?

INTERVIEWER: What do you think the value proposition is?

CANDIDATE: I thought a little bit about the Honey Nut Cheerios before I flew out for the interview. I've always loved Cheerios because it's tasty. And my parents liked that I was eating it because the whole grain oats made it healthy.

INTERVIEWER: Bingo. The TV ads are focused on the core value prop of taste and healthy. We were known in the 90s for commercials where Buzz, our bee character, would tempt kids with Honey Nut Cheerios. At first, kids would refuse, but eventually they would give in after Buzz told them there was real honey.

Our latest TV ads update this message with more contemporary flair. We utilize the latest hip-hop song from Nelly, "Ride Wit Me." The chorus uses the Cheerios tagline, "Must be the honey."

CANDIDATE: Thanks for the context.

Candidate writes the components of the Big Picture framework on the whiteboard:

- *Business goal: increase revenue five percent this year*
- *Marketing goal*
- *Segmentation*
- *Targeting*
- *Positioning*
- *4P's – promotions, place, price and product*

CANDIDATE: Okay, here's how I'd like to proceed before we get to the promotional tactics. I'd like to clarify the marketing objective, be clear on which segment we're going to target and the positioning statement.

From there, we'll talk about promotional tactics and how they influence distribution, product / packaging and price, if at all.

INTERVIEWER: Sounds like a good plan. Jump in.

Candidate writes on the board:

- *Awareness*
- *Interest*
- *Trial*
- *Purchase*

CANDIDATE: Let's start with the marketing objective. I believe Honey Nut Cheerios is one of the top three cereal brands today. I imagine its awareness is very strong, so let's rule out awareness as a top marketing objective.

In terms of interest, adults, especially Millennials, love it. Kids like it too. But I could also see that kids think that Honey Nut Cheerios is the "cereal that their parents eat." In other words, it's not cool anymore. Am I right?

INTERVIEWER: Yes.

CANDIDATE: My research tells me that Cheerios' sales are growing at about 3 percent per year. I feel purchases should be our marketing objective and here's why: I've always wondered why I would restrict myself to eating Honey Nut Cheerios during breakfast. I think it would make a great afternoon snack. It's healthy and tasty.

INTERVIEWER: Sounds like a worthy goal and an interesting insight.

CANDIDATE: With something like this, we're trying to drum up additional demand and increase purchase occasions, especially with our existing customer base.

Candidate writes on the board:

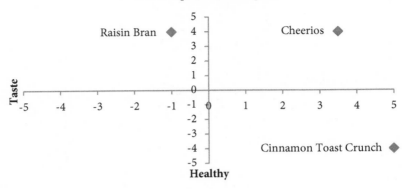

Perceptual Map

Rise Above the Noise

CANDIDATE: Let's jump into segmentation. Cheerios is perceived to be tasty and healthy, so we'll place it in the upper right. I'm not a cereal expert, but let's say the competitors are Cinnamon Toast Crunch, which is known to be tasty, but clearly not as healthy with all that sugar. Raisin Bran is not tasty, but very healthy.

We'll have the best shot at winning the marketing battle if we go for segments that care about the upper right, where Cheerios is currently positioned. The first segment that comes to mind is parents. As a collective, they're not as health conscious as the yoga adults, who are willing to sacrifice taste for health. For parents, life is too hard to just eat cereal that tastes like cardboard.

INTERVIEWER: I'm good with parents.

CANDIDATE: Do you want me to discuss the value prop?

INTERVIEWER: No need. You've got the gist. We're the healthy cereal that tastes good.

CANDIDATE: I'll go with that. Before proceeding, a quick summary on where we're at:

Candidate writes the following:

Promotional plan

- *Goal: increase sales by five percent.*
- *Marketing objective: remove blockers to additional Honey Nut Cheerios purchases. This will bubble desire to eat the cereal beyond breakfast.*
- *Source of volume: grow category.*
- *Target customer: adults that emphasize healthy snacks.*
- *Value prop: healthy cereal that tastes great.*

CANDIDATE: Here are the elements of my plan:

- *Product.* I would like to launch a new SKU focused on Honey Nut Cheerios as a snack. For lack of a better name, we can call it Honey Nut Cheerios Snack Bits. I would package them as 100-calorie packs, consisting of eight ounces each.
- *Marketing Channels.* I would target locations where healthy adults are. Here are a few examples:
  - *Partner with gyms.* Giveaway the product to gym members who have just completed their workout and want a healthy treat.
  - *Partner with corporations.* Giveaway the product to corporate workers who are health-conscious, such as those living on West coast cities.
- *Sales Channels.* I'd focus on retail channels where we have a strong presence, such as grocery stores, mass merchandisers, drug stores, convenience stores and club stores. It would be ideal to target organic grocery stores, such as Whole Foods.

However, we're unlikely to have relationships with them, so I think we can pass.

- *Promotions.* For the brand launch, I'd acquire $20 to $50 million for a TV advertising campaign. We can go into more detail, but I think TV stations that target healthy eating, such as the Food Network and National Geographic. I'd also want to target prime time ad spots on network channels such as ABC, CBS and NBC. I'd also consider targeted video ads on YouTube.
- *Pricing.* I'd choose pricing levels that are similar to competitors.

Scorecard

Overall Rating	Excellent
Marketing Aptitude	Above Average
Plan	Excellent
Communication Skills	Excellent
Composure	Excellent
Satisfying Conclusion	Excellent

Comments

The candidate did a faithful job of applying the Big Picture framework. He also did a good job of understanding customers' needs. The idea to create Snack Bits is unique and intriguing. It makes sense for a lot of reasons: the younger adult segment is aware of the Honey Nut Cheerios brand and the "healthy and tasty" value proposition.

But here's why the candidate received an "above average" for marketing aptitude: The candidate rightly capitalizes on a trend: adults' desire for healthy eating. However, the suggestion seems out of left field. It would be easier to accept if it was compared with other new product introduction ideas. Also, the prompt indicated the brand's goal of increasing revenue five percent within one year. There's not enough time to launch a new product and see meaningful revenues in just twelve months. An excellent response would have suggested more reasonable tactics such as advertising, trade promotions or price discounts.

Develop a social good campaign for Teavana.

CANDIDATE: I've been to Teavana, but it's been a while. I'd like to check my understanding of the company with you.

INTERVIEWER: Go for it.

CANDIDATE: Teavana is a tea retailer with more than 300 locations in the United States, Canada and Mexico. Teavana is known for high quality teas and unique product assortment. For example, its top seller is a citrus, lavender and sage tea blend followed by a strawberry, rose champagne and peach tea blend.

INTERVIEWER: Sounds on point to me.

CANDIDATE: When it comes to Teavana's social values, I know Teavana hires women in developing countries and follows fair labor standards. The women also create tea tumblers, with $3 in proceeds going to CARE, a non-profit organization that fights poverty.

INTERVIEWER: Sounds right to me.

CANDIDATE: I'd like to approach the question in two parts: strategy and tactics. For strategy, I'd like to understand the company's overall business objectives, marketing goals and target segments.

For tactics, I found the following framework on your company website for developing social campaigns:

- Clarify social values
- Define the mission statement
- Create visibility by partnering with the right organizations
- Drive action

Unless you'd like me to do otherwise, I'll use that tactical framework.

INTERVIEWER: Sounds good.

CANDIDATE: In the interest of time, would you like me to cover all parts, or do you just want me to focus on the second part — creating the social campaign tactics?

INTERVIEWER: We have enough time. Go ahead and cover both parts of the plan.

CANDIDATE: Starting from the business objective, the biggest goal is to drive more sales revenue. Are there any other objectives I should consider, such as market share?

INTERVIEWER: Nope, that sounds right.

CANDIDATE: To achieve the business objective, we need to think about the marketing goal. When I think about my own Teavana experiences, I love it. But a lot of my friends aren't Teavana customers. They are aware of the brand, but they don't make any purchases.

Based on my personal experiences, we should focus on an acquisition, not a retention campaign. And if we think back on the marketing funnel — awareness, interest, trial and purchase — I feel Teavana's biggest marketing challenge is trial. Anytime I drag a girlfriend into the Teavana store, they usually end up purchasing two bags of tea. They just need to try one sample to be hooked.

INTERVIEWER: Continue.

CANDIDATE: From a segmentation perspective, we can segment Teavana customers in many different ways. We could segment based on:

- Price sensitivity: price elastic vs. inelastic
- Demographic: young professionals in their 20s or baby boomers in their 50s and 60s

- Lifestyle: health-conscious yoga crowd or in-touch-with-nature granola crowd

Do you have a preference?

INTERVIEWER: Nope, I'll leave it up to you.

CANDIDATE: I'll keep things simple and target a specific demographic: young professionals in their 20s. I'm assuming Teavana doesn't have problems with their existing customer base. They're very loyal and a reliable word-of-mouth marketing channel. The issue is attracting new customers, especially segments that are more accustomed to drinking other refreshments such as coffee and fruit smoothies.

INTERVIEWER: So what's the value proposition to this segment?

CANDIDATE: I'll break from the conventional value proposition template and use a tagline to convey the sentiment:

The short version: Nourish the body, nourish the world.

The long version: The finest, all-natural teas to nourish your body while empowering friends around the world.

INTERVIEWER: I don't understand the part about "empowering friends around the world." What does that mean?

CANDIDATE: It acknowledges our social mission — our commitment to organic, fair trade teas while investing our revenue into social causes, such as empowering women in developing countries.

INTERVIEWER: Your explanation makes sense, but your long version tagline is rough. I do like the short version. The rhythmic repetition makes it easy-to-remember, and the word choice "nourish" is unique and appropriate.

CANDIDATE: This is a good segue into your agency's social campaign framework. Our product value is about high quality tea, and our social value is empowering women around the world — developing countries or not.

INTERVIEWER: What's the mission statement?

CANDIDATE: Give me 30 seconds to brainstorm something.

The mission statement is "Hundred. Hundred. Hundred." or:

- Educate 100 million women
- Provide 100 thousand new jobs
- Create 100 new woman-led businesses

INTERVIEWER: I like it. It's bold, inspirational and memorable.

CANDIDATE: Some of the organizations I would partner with include:

- *Education.* Anita Borg Institute for Women and Technology, DonorsChoose
- *Careers.* Dress for Success, Wider Opportunities for Women
- *Entrepreneurship.* Women's Global Empowerment Fund

INTERVIEWER: What's the Women's Global Empowerment Fund?

CANDIDATE: They reach out to underserved women in northern Uganda, empower them with microloans and help Ugandan women start businesses.

INTERVIEWER: Okay, we're running short on time. What are your two main tactics for driving action?

CANDIDATE: Here are my top two:

1. Create a competition where female entrepreneurs can receive business loans and mentorship from top female executives. Ask

each participating company to invest $1 million into our social campaign. Some female execs that I have in mind include:

    a.   Sheryl Sandberg, Facebook COO

    b.   Indra Nooyi, CEO of PepsiCo

    c.   Ellen Kullman, CEO of DuPont

2. Drive Teavana's Millennials to participate in a DonorsChoose-like campaign. Have them donate money where students can buy the school supplies they need. Teavana will offer a $1 match for every $2 contributed. In return, the students will write notes about their education progress and how the supplies made a difference in their learning.

INTERVIEWER: Thank you.

Scorecard

Overall Rating	Excellent
Marketing Aptitude	Excellent
Plan	Excellent
Communication Skills	Excellent
Composure	Excellent
Satisfying Conclusion	Excellent

Comments

This is an extraordinary response. Rarely does an interviewer see a response of this caliber.

The response shows that the candidate has done his homework in advance about the brand, the agency and the campaign. He demonstrates creativity and sincere passion. He also demonstrated some dexterity in blending the Big Picture framework with the agency's social marketing framework.

How would you market Google AdWords?

CANDIDATE: Here's how I think of marketing plans.

Candidate draws the Big Picture framework

First, we define the business goal and marketing objective. I'd then consider the potential segments we could target. I'd define the positioning statement and then plan out the marketing tactics, which might include pricing and distribution.

For our goal, we could try to maximize profits, revenue or market share. In preparation for this interview, I've read blogs from online advertising pundits. They say that Google has been trying to get more small businesses to try AdWords. Digging a little deeper, small businesses have heard of AdWords and know it's effective with generating leads. However, they've never had time to actually try it. I'd recommend that we drive AdWords acquisition, with an emphasis of getting new customers to spend at least $100.

Next, we need to pick a segment. There are different types of small businesses out there, such as dry cleaners and plumbers. Google executives admit that AdWords is not easy to use, so it makes sense to target technically savvy advertisers. Some ways to target technically savvy customers include targeting small business owners who use Intuit QuickBooks or have setup their own website.

Now that we've identified a target audience, we need a positioning statement. Here is mine:

For small business owners who would like to get more leads, Google AdWords advertises your products or services when consumers are looking to buy. Unlike other advertising methods, AdWords is the only kind that provides traceable ROI, ensuring that every dollar spent converts to sales.

Let's now discuss promotional tactics. Give me a moment to brainstorm.

INTERVIWER: Sure.

CANDIDATE: There's a large number of tactics that we can try, but here are three that come to the top of my head:

We can do a co-marketing campaign with Intuit. It could be an email or direct mail campaign to Intuit's QuickBooks customers, inviting them to join an AdWords webinar. For those that attend, we can offer a $75 voucher to try AdWords.

We can also do a similar co-marketing campaign (webinar & voucher) with hosting companies such as GoDaddy.

Lastly, we can partner with office supply stores, such as Staples and Office Depot, for AdWords displays that demonstrate how AdWords works.

Here's why I recommended these three tactics. First, they focus on our target customer. Second, many of the tactics have a demonstration component, which is ideal for complicated products. Lastly, all three tactics have an incentive to sign up and use the product.

Finally, I would measure the effectiveness of the campaign by looking at the cost per acquisition, the number of acquisitions attained and the amount of revenue from each new acquisition.

Scorecard

Overall Rating	Excellent
Marketing Aptitude	Above Average
Plan	Excellent
Communication Skills	Excellent
Composure	Excellent
Satisfying Conclusion	Excellent

Comments

Candidate offers a thoughtful response to building an AdWords campaign. The justification at the end of the response was a very nice touch that we haven't seen from other candidates.

How would you market Halos?

CANDIDATE: What are Halos?

INTERVIEWER: They are a type of clementine from California. They look like miniature oranges.

CANDIDATE: Ah, I've had those before. They're easy to peel.

INTERVIEWER: They're also marketed as sweet and seedless.

CANDIDATE: I suppose Halos are positioning themselves against regular navel oranges, which aren't always sweet, seedless or easy to peel.

INTERVIEWER: Bingo.

CANDIDATE: I have a couple more follow-up questions. Who's the target customer?

INTERVIEWER: Kids and moms. Kids like Halos because they fit in their hands and are something they can peel. Moms like Halos because eating fruit is a lot better than eating processed food.

CANDIDATE: Who's the competition?

INTERVIEWER: There's a long list of competitors, but the primary market leader is Cuties. Ironically, Halos' owners, Lynda and Stewart Resnick used to be co-owners of Cuties. However, due to a business dispute, the Resnicks sold Cuties to their former business partner.

CANDIDATE: Are the products perceived as different?

INTERVIEWER: To be honest, no. From the packaging, you can tell that both Cuties and Halos trumpet the seedless and easy-to-peel nature of the products.

I'll give you another insight. Mommy bloggers have asked whether there are differences between Cuties and Halos, and they can't figure it out either. Some Halos fans cite its non-GMO status; that is, Halos are not genetically modified. However, non-GMO certification is something Cuties is pursuing and likely to achieve.

CANDIDATE: What's GMO?

INTERVIEWER: GMO stands for "genetically modified organism."

CANDIDATE: I would think that lack of competitive differentiation is the main problem when competing with Cuties.

INTERVIEWER: That's correct.

CANDIDATE: Are there other elements I should investigate such as distribution channels, relative pricing and promotional activity?

INTERVIEWER: Those are good questions. But for the sake of time, let's say competitive differentiation is the main need. Can you provide the recommended plan of attack?

CANDIDATE: Give me a moment to collect my thoughts and summarize my recommendation.

Candidate takes 90 seconds

CANDIDATE: Halos is a new clementine brand. Its main competitor is Cuties, the current market leader. For the sake of time, you asked me to focus specifically on creating competitive differentiation between Halos and Cuties.

Giving it some thought, I feel the biggest opportunity is to make the core product, clementines, different. As far as I know there's no option to grow clementines to be sweeter or smaller. And to grow them in different colors, I'd doubt consumers will find a purple clementine appealing. So here are my ideas on how to make Halos clementines better:

Make it easier to peel

YumScrubBlog.com

ThriftyFun.com

Building on the core benefit of easy-to-peel, Halos may apply a food dye that helps kids peel the clementine in different ways, including the corkscrew and a star shape.

Make it educational

Print different educational messages on the clementines. Here are some ideas:

1. Numbers
2. Letters
3. Images

Make it fun

The company can also print fun messages including:

1. Juggling instructions
2. Fortune telling

Make it decorative

School Bites

Print decorative designs that appeal to kids. For instance, a set of pumpkins.

INTERVIEWER: Thanks.

Scorecard

Overall Rating	Excellent
Marketing Aptitude	Excellent

Plan	Excellent
Communication Skills	Excellent
Composure	Excellent
Satisfying Conclusion	Excellent

Comments

The candidate did an excellent job zeroing in on competitive differentiation as the main problem. While curious about pricing, distribution and other aspects of the business, he heeded the interviewer's guidance and kept focused on the competitive differentiation problem. Showcasing several different ideas can be more compelling than just sharing one. It demonstrates creativity. It also protects the candidate from presenting a single, lackluster idea.

Chapter 4 Pricing

Questions about price are about determining if candidates can diagnose a business situation, formulate a methodical way of tackling it and make a concrete decision.

Generally, there are two types of pricing questions: pricing a new product or changing the price of an existing product.

What is the Interviewer Looking For?

Pricing is one of the most important levers in the marketing mix. Interviewers use pricing questions to evaluate a candidate's business judgment.

A thoughtful answer will highlight a candidate's understanding of:

- Pricing fundamentals
- Buyer psychology
- Market strategy
- Competitive dynamics
- Supply and demand fundamentals

It can also test a candidate's ability to manipulate numbers, especially with questions about changing prices of an existing product, where a candidate needs to compare profits before and after a change.

How to Approach the Question

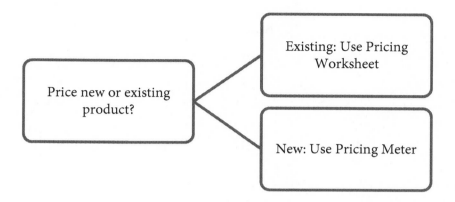

Rise Above the Noise

I've created this decision tree to help you determine how to tackle a pricing question. If it's an existing product, use breakeven analysis. If it's a new product, use the pricing meter, described in more detail below.

Changing Price of an Existing Product

When it comes to evaluating a price change to an existing product, analyze the total profit before and after the change. To keep things organized, here's a worksheet that helps me collect necessary inputs and organize my calculations. I call it the Pricing Worksheet.

Pricing Worksheet

	Old	New
Price		
Cost Per Unit		
Gross Profit Per Unit		
Unit Volume		
Gross Profit		

Rise Above the Noise

Remember that a competitive response to your price change can shift your demand curve, forcing you to recalculate profit impact from a price change.

Determining Price of a New Product

Pricing new products is a little different from changing pricing of existing products. It's hard to predict demand for new products. Granted, you could survey respondents on their willingness to purchase at a particular price, but that data is inherently unreliable. You could also do some pilots in smaller markets and extrapolate those results to a domestic or international launch.

Long story short, when asked to price a new product, it's more likely to be a qualitative discussion around pricing products.

When it comes to new product pricing, keep three numbers in mind: the customer's willingness to pay, the price of competitive products and the cost to produce. This comes together in what I call the Pricing Meter.

Pricing Meter

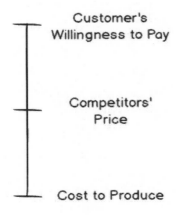

Rise Above the Noise

The cost to produce is the lowest price most companies would want to charge for their product. It's the absolute minimum necessary to cover the variable costs. Some companies are well aware of their cost to produce, or COGS, and enforce a cost-plus pricing, where they apply a standard margin on their costs to charge their customers a final price.

There are times when companies sell for less than COGS. This is called a loss-leader strategy. In this case, brands attempt to sell below cost (or market price) in an effort to win market share.

The customer's willingness to pay is the highest price customers are willing to pay. This number is usually their next best alternative. For some, this might be the price of building a similar solution from scratch. For others, it might be the price of tolerating an unsolved problem. For instance, the price of not getting a child a McDonald's Happy Meal might be an unhappy child. Hard to put a price on that situation, but given the alternative, a parent might be willing to pay $50 to have a happy child, despite the fact that a Happy Meal might cost $3 to produce.

The final number to consider is somewhere between the low number (the cost to produce) and the high number (the customer's willingness to pay.) And that's the competitor's or market price. It's price of the next best alternative that consumers determine to be a decent substitute for the other. For example, many consider Coke and Pepsi to be near perfect substitutes. As a result, Coke pays attention to pricing their products within a reasonable cost to Pepsi.

Practice Questions

1. Should Hidden Valley increase the price of its ranch dressing?
2. Should you raise prices for Pringles?
3. Delta just announced a 10 percent across-the-board price cut. As United Airlines, do you stay or follow?

4. Should AT&T implement a new return policy for new cell phone purchases?
5. Should Best Buy change its return policy from 15 to 90 days?

Answers

Should Hidden Valley increase the price of its ranch dressing?

INTERVIEWER: Should Hidden Valley increase the price of its ranch dressing from $2.99 to $3.50?

CANDIDATE: When evaluating a price increase, I'd like to assess profitability. Is there anything else you'd like me to address?

INTERVIEWER: No.

CANDIDATE: Great, I'd like to collect some information from you first. How much does it cost to make Hidden Valley ranch dressing?

INTERVIEWER: Let's say $1 per bottle.

CANDIDATE: Thanks. I'll assume the cost of goods sold is the same under the old and new price. How many units are we selling per year?

INTERVIEWER: 10 million bottles.

CANDIDATE: How many bottles do we expect to sell after the price increase?

INTERVIEWER: 9 million bottles.

CANDIDATE: Do we expect any competitive responses that might force us to revise our sales projections?

INTERVIEWER: That's a reasonable insight. But for the sake of time, please calculate a profitability number and make a recommendation, based on what you have so far.

CANDIDATE: Okay, give me a minute to make some calculations.

Candidate writes the following on the whiteboard

	Old	New
Price	$2.99	$3.50
Cost Per Unit	$1	$1
Gross Profit Per Unit	$1.99	$2.50
Unit Volume	10 million	9 million
Gross Profit	$19.9 million	$22.5 million

CANDIDATE: Based on my calculations, Hidden Valley will make an additional $2.6 million from the price increase. The price should be increased.

Scorecard

Overall Rating	Excellent
Marketing Aptitude	Excellent
Plan	Excellent
Communication Skills	Excellent
Composure	Excellent
Satisfying Conclusion	Excellent

Comments

In this quick pricing question, the interviewer's intent is to assess the candidate's analytical ability, problem solving skills and composure. You can see that the candidate, aided by the Pricing Worksheet, tackled the question effortlessly.

Should you raise prices for Pringles?

INTERVIEWER: You are the brand manager for Pringles potato chips. Your boss wants to improve profitability to increase price. Should you do it?

CANDIDATE: This is for the American market, right?

INTERVIEWER: Yes.

CANDIDATE: What's Pringles' current price?

INTERVIEWER: $1.99 per can.

CANDIDATE: And how many did they sell last year?

INTERVIEWER: 300 million cans.

CANDIDATE: How much does he want to raise the price?

INTERVIEWER: Five percent.

CANDIDATE: And if we raise price, how will that affect volume?

INTERVIEWER: The annual growth rate, in terms of units sold, will decrease from four percent to one percent.

CANDIDATE: Okay, let me do some quick math.

Candidate writes the following

*$2 per can * 300 million cans sold * 1.04 growth rate = $624 million*

*$2 per can * 1.05 price increase * 300 million cans * 1.01 growth rate = $636.3 million*

CANDIDATE: Based on my calculations, Pringles can increase its revenue from $624 million to $636 million by increasing price by five percent. However, the competition could respond by changing their prices, in either direction. A competitive move could affect demand for our products, and we would have to revise our forecast for a more accurate estimate.

INTERVIEWER: Who do you think are Pringles' main competitors?

CANDIDATE: Here are the potato chip manufacturers I can think off the top of my head: Lay's, Ruffles, Kettle Chips and Pop Chips.

INTERVIEWER: For simplicity, let's say Lay's is the only competitor whose moves can affect Pringles' demand.

CANDIDATE: Do you have more information on what competitive responses Lay's is considering?

INTERVIEWER: If Pringles keeps the prices same, Lay's will keep the prices the same.

However, if Pringles increases prices, then there's no chance that Lay's would raise prices. However, there's a 15 percent chance that Lay's would keep prices the same, and there's an 85 percent chance that Lay's would actually reduce prices by five percent.

CANDIDATE: How would Lay's price reduction affect Pringles' volume?

INTERVIEWER: It would decrease volume by eight percent.

Okay, let me recalculate the numbers, based on the likely scenario that Lay's will decrease prices.

Candidate writes the following:

*$2 per can * 1.05 price increase * 300 million cans * .92 growth rate = $579.6 million*

CANDIDATE: After factoring in Lay's most likely competitive response, Pringles revenue will be $579.6 million, which is worse than the anticipated $624 million if Pringles decided not to increase price. Given this information, I would recommend that Pringles not increase prices.

Scorecard

Overall Rating	Above Average
Marketing Aptitude	Excellent
Plan	Excellent
Communication Skills	Above Average
Composure	Excellent
Satisfying Conclusion	Excellent

Comments

This example shows how a competitive response would lead a candidate to recalculate his profitability projections and reverse his initial belief that Pringles should raise prices. Using the Profit Worksheet would have organized the candidate's calculations, making it easier to follow:

Revenue Impact on Price Change

	Old	New
Price	$2	$2.10
Cost Per Unit	N/A	N/A
Gross Profit Per Unit	N/A	N/A
Unit Volume	312 million	303 million
Gross Revenue	$624 million	$636.3 million

Revenue Impact on Price Change, After Competitive Response

	Old	New
Price	$2	$2.10
Cost Per Unit	N/A	N/A
Gross Profit Per Unit	N/A	N/A
Unit Volume	312 million	276 million
Gross Revenue	$624 million	$579.6 million

Delta just announced a 10 percent across-the-board price cut. As United Airlines, do you stay or follow?

CANDIDATE: How much volume did Delta gain?

INTERVIEWER: Two percent.

CANDIDATE: What's the impact of the price cut to United?

INTERVIEWER: Volume has dropped three percent.

CANDIDATE: How many tickets does United usually sell in a week?

INTERVIEWER: About one million.

CANDIDATE: And what's the average price per ticket?

INTERVIEWER: $405.

CANDIDATE: Doing some quick math, assuming United and Delta don't make any changes, United is going to lose $12.2 million this week.

INTERVIEWER: Thanks for crunching the numbers. Just taking a step back, what do you think is the biggest industry concern?

CANDIDATE: Other competitors in the industry are concerned about the prisoner's dilemma, a game theory concept that describes why parties might not cooperate when it is in their best interest to do so.

In this case, if United Airlines also matches the fare cuts, then the rest of the industry will have to cut prices so that they don't lose demand. They'll be most concerned in markets where demand is inelastic. Had they cooperated and not lowered prices, all the airlines will sell the same number of tickets for higher prices. Price fixing is illegal, but we'll set that aside for now.

INTERVIEWER: Do you think it makes sense for United to do an across-the-board price cut?

CANDIDATE: Well, it's unlikely that the across-the-board price cuts will affect United's markets equally.

INTERVIEWER: Why is that?

CANDIDATE: Delta doesn't compete in certain United markets.

INTERVIEWER: Give me an example.

CANDIDATE: Let's take a major United hub like San Francisco. Delta may have a few routes going in and out, perhaps from major Delta hubs like Atlanta and Salt Lake City, but they don't have a lot. So while consumers might like Delta's price cuts, there are a limited number of seats. People who need to travel, like business people, will continue to pay higher fares.

INTERVIEWER: What do you recommend that United do?

CANDIDATE: I recommend that United analyze the impact of Delta's price cuts on a market-by-market basis. And wait to see if the rest of the industry follows with the price cuts.

If so, we'll have to cut because our customers will have reasonable substitutes of what will then be higher fares. If we do cut, we should cut on a market-by-market basis so that we don't unnecessarily impact our profits.

If the market doesn't follow, then it's reasonable that Delta has to roll back the price reductions. We can go into the math, but my guess is a 10 percent across-the-board price cut might help in the short-term. That is, the marginal revenue will exceed the marginal cost. However, in the longer-term, it's unlikely that the average revenue, from the price cut, will exceed average cost.

Scorecard

Overall Rating	Excellent
Marketing Aptitude	Excellent
Plan	Excellent
Communication Skills	Excellent
Composure	Excellent
Satisfying Conclusion	Excellent

Comments

This pricing question unfolds differently from the previous examples. There is some number crunching, but the interviewer is more interested in a qualitative discussion. The candidate does a good job discussing some of the more subtle nuances of pricing including prisoner's dilemma, inelastic demand and selective price cuts by market. The candidate also references concepts from beginners' economics, such as marginal revenue exceeding marginal cost.

Overall, the candidate's conversational tone and thoughtful discussion made his response enjoyable for the interviewer while exuding credibility that he can do the job.

Should AT&T implement a new return policy for new cell phone purchases?

INTERVIEWER: AT&T has a 14 day return policy for new cell phone purchases. AT&T is considering a 90 day return policy. Should AT&T do it?

CANDIDATE: To determine whether AT&T should do it, I'll calculate the incremental revenue from the initiative. Is there anything else I should factor in?

INTERVIEWER: Nope. That sounds like a good plan.

CANDIDATE: Okay, give me a moment to collect my thoughts.

Candidate takes 45 seconds to sketch the following

	Old	New
Policy	14 day return	90 day return
Revenue		
Gross margin		
Gross profit		
Fixed costs		
Variable costs		
Net profit		

CANDIDATE: To calculate net profit, here's some data I'd like to collect from you.

INTERVIEWER: Sure, ask away.

After some back and forth questions as well as a couple of calculations, the candidate produces the following table:

	Old	New
Policy	14 day return	90 day return
Revenue	20 billion	22 billion
Gross margin	50%	50%
Gross profit	10 billion	11 billion
Fixed costs	-200 million	-300 million
Variable costs	Negligible	Negligible
Net profit	9.8 billion	10.7 billion

* Annual numbers

CANDIDATE: The new plan will generate 10.7 billion vs. 9.8 billion. AT&T should do it.

Scorecard

Overall Rating	Excellent
Marketing Aptitude	Excellent
Plan	Excellent
Communication Skills	Excellent
Composure	Excellent
Satisfying Conclusion	Excellent

Comments

Once the candidate has all the numbers, the calculations are straightforward. This question is included in the pricing section because similar to pricing questions, the impact of this return policy requires a break-even calculation approach that's similar to other pricing questions.

Should Best Buy change its return policy from 15 to 90 days?

CANDIDATE: Why is Best Buy considering a change to its return policy?

INTERVIEWER: Best Buy executives have seen other retailers succeed with more lenient return policies. Costco and Wal-Mart have a 90-day return policy.

CANDIDATE: And I'm assuming they're hoping an increased return rate will drive higher revenues?

INTERVIEWER: Yes, the point of the exercise is to calculate the breakeven order size under a 90-day return rule.

CANDIDATE: Give me a moment to collect my thoughts.

	Old	New
Policy	15 day return	90 day return
Return rate		
Number of customers		
Orders per customer		
Average order size		Unknown
Gross margin		
Gross profit		
Returns per customer		
Loss per return		
Total return loss		
Fixed costs		
Addtl. variable costs		
Net profit		

CANDIDATE: Here's the information and calculations I need to determine the average order size to make this profitable. So let's jump in. My first question: What is Best Buy's current return rate?

INTERVIEWER: 20 percent.

CANDIDATE: If they change to a 90-day policy, how much will the return rate go up?

INTERVIEWER: 30 percent.

CANDIDATE: How many customers do they have under the old and new policy?

INTERVIEWER: They currently have 30 million customers a year. We expect it to go up to 33 million in the new policy.

CANDIDATE: How often do customers order each year?

INTERVIEWER: Under the old policy, about three times a year. Under the new policy, we expect ordering to increase to four times a year.

CANDIDATE: How much do they buy each time they purchase?

INTERVIEWER: $500 under the old policy.

CANDIDATE: How about the new policy?

INTERVIEWER: That's for you to figure out, remember?

CANDIDATE: That's right. How often do customers do return purchases, and how much do we lose from returns?

INTERVIEWER: Here's the information you requested:

	Old	New
Returns per customer	0.6	1.2
Loss per return	-$50	-$100

CANDIDATE: Are there any fixed costs with rolling out a 90-day change?

INTERVIEWER: In reality, there's a $2 million one-time charge for rolling out the 90-day program. It includes promotion, training and process re-engineering. There's also an additional $5 million annual expense for increased staff to process returns.

However, for your calculations, these charges will be inconsequential, so no need to include them.

CANDIDATE: That's all the information I need. Give me a moment to work through my calculations.

Candidate writes the following on the whiteboard

	Old	New
Policy	15 day return	90 day return
Return rate	20%	30%
Number of customers	30 million	33 million
Orders per customer	3	4
Average order size	$500	Unknown

Gross margin	50%	50%
Gross profit	$22.5 billion	To be calculated
Returns per customer	0.6	1.2
Loss per return	-$50	-$100
Total return loss	-$900 million	-$3.96 billion
Fixed costs	$0	Negligible
Addtl. variable costs	$0	Negligible
Net profit	$21.6 billion	>= $21.6 billion

Old net profit =< New net profit

Old net profit =< New gross profit + New return loss

Old net profit =< (New number of customers) * (New orders per customer) * (New average order size) * (New gross margin) + New return loss

New average order size >= [(Old net profit) – (New return loss)]/ [(New number of customers) * (New orders per customer) * (New gross margin)]

New average order size = $387.27

CANDIDATE: Based on my calculations, the return loss will grow from $900 million to $3.96 billion.

To break even, each customer would have to purchase $387.27 per order.

INTERVIEWER: Thanks for the calculations, so what would you recommend?

CANDIDATE: I would recommend that Best Buy pursue the longer 90-day return policy. Based on the assumptions we're given, it's very likely that Best Buy can break even and possibly increase its revenues.

INTERVIEWER: Thanks.

Scorecard

Overall Rating	Excellent
Marketing Aptitude	Excellent
Plan	Excellent
Communication Skills	Excellent
Composure	Excellent
Satisfying Conclusion	Excellent

Comments

Bravo. This is a flawless response. This question is one of the more challenging, lengthier break-even questions any candidate would see at the market interview, and the candidate handled it with aplomb. This is a top 1% response.

Chapter 5 Declining Sales

Declining sales is a common marketing interview question, especially at brand management companies. Some examples:

- Why did Kit Kat sales decline year-over-year?
- Colgate toothpaste sales are flat, but market share declined. What happened?

What is the Interviewer Looking For?

- *Problem solving skills.* Do you have a logical and efficient way of approaching the problem?
- *Business judgment.* How keen is your business judgment? How quickly can you find the issue and propose relevant solutions?
- *Creativity.* Do you have unique and memorable ideas that are relevant to improving the business goal?

How to Approach the Question

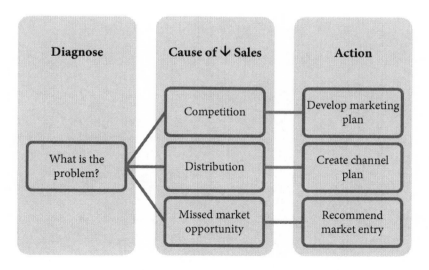

Rise Above the Noise

I'd recommend approaching questions about declining sales in two parts:

1. What is the problem?
2. What's your recommended solution to the problem?

For your diagnosis, remember:

Sales = Price * Quantity

Ask questions that reveal how price and sales quantity have been affected. Here are potential questions to ask:

- Has customer demand been affected lately?
  - Changing consumer preferences?
  - Reformulate an existing product?
- Did the competition make any changes?
  - Launch a new product?
  - Lower prices?
  - Increase advertising?
- Have our channels been affected?
  - Lose shelf space?
  - Reduce channel promotions?
- What other changes have occurred?

After a couple questions, the cause of the declining sales will be clear. It may be a competitive issue, a distribution problem or a missed market opportunity.

From there, you'll have to recommend a course of action. Depending on the problem, you can use an appropriate framework. For instance, if the problem is with competition, the Big Picture marketing framework is appropriate.

Practice Questions

1. As Brand Manager for Kingsford Charcoal, how do you increase sales in a shrinking market?

2. Kit Kat sales declined year-over-year. Why is that, and what would you do to address it?

3. Colgate toothpaste sales are flat, but market share has gone down. What happened and how would you improve it?

Answers

As Brand Manager for Kingsford Charcoal, how do you increase sales in a shrinking market?

INTERVIEWER: You are the Brand Manager for Kingsford Charcoal. Gas grill usage is substantially increasing, leading charcoal to decline. What should you do?

CANDIDATE: Before I jump in, can I ask for some background information? I don't know much about the charcoal market.

INTERVIEWER: Sure.

CANDIDATE: Who are Kingsford's major competitors, and what is their market share?

INTERVIEWER: Kingsford's top competitors are Royal Oak charcoal followed by several private label brands. Here are the latest market share figures:

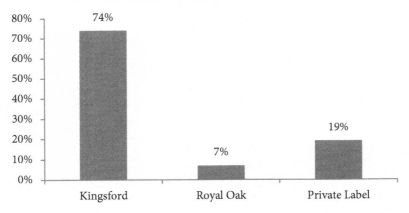

Charcoal Market Share in the Last 12 Months

Rise Above the Noise

CANDIDATE: It looks like Kingsford is the dominant charcoal player today. Has that always been the case?

INTERVIEWER: Yes, Kingsford's market share has been roughly in the 75% range for the last 20 years.

CANDIDATE: Is it fair to say Kingsford has weathered the private label onslaught well?

INTERVIEWER: Yes. Even though Kingsford is priced at a premium, consumers are willing to pay a $3 to $4 premium for a known brand.

CANDIDATE: How about consumer trends? When I go to BBQ parties, I see more gas than charcoal grills.

INTERVIEWER: Yes, gas grills have become more popular over the years. Here's some recent data on gas vs. charcoal trends. Electric grills are also a significant player in the market, but let's set them aside for the purpose of simplicity.

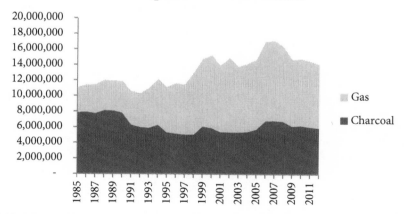

Grill Shipments in North America

CANDIDATE: It appears consumer preferences have changed over time. What explains the growth of gas grills over charcoal ones?

INTERVIEWER: What do you think?

CANDIDATE: A couple of reasons pop in mind:

- *Speed*. Gas grills can heat up within 10 to 15 minutes, whereas a charcoal fire could take 30 minutes to heat up.
- *Messy*. Charcoal is dirty, and lighter fluid, if tipped over, can create a mess.
- *Ease of use*. Charcoal grills can be hard to light.
- *Safety*. Charcoal grills are more likely to pose a threat to nearby buildings.
- *Heating control and consistency*. It's easier to get a gas grill to heat up to a particular temperature, especially with knob controls.

INTERVIEWER: Sounds like you've covered most of the reasons.

CANDIDATE: Do charcoal grills have advantages over gas grills?

INTERVIEWER: Based on some recent barbecue association data, here are reasons why consumers like charcoal grills:

- 77 percent like the taste of charcoal grills
- 46 percent like cooking outdoors
- 35 percent like entertaining
- 32 percent think it's inexpensive
- 30 percent think it's easier and more convenient

We also found that during tailgate parties, charcoal grills are used 76 percent of the time. Gas grills are used only 24 percent of the time.

Charcoal grills produce a different (and some claim, better) smoke than gas grills. Using smoke vs. flame heat is a trend that's gaining in popularity.

CANDIDATE: What has Kingsford done so far to promote the perceived flavor advantages of charcoal over gas grilling?

INTERVIEWER: We have several SKUs that promote unique flavors. This is packaging for our Mesquite SKU. We also have a Hickory SKU.

CANDIDATE: Thanks for answering my questions and providing helpful background context. Is there anything else I should know before I summarize my recommendation to you?

INTERVIEWER: No, I can't think of anything.

CANDIDATE: Give me a few moments to prepare my recommendation

Candidate takes 60 seconds

CANDIDATE: To summarize, Kingsford is dominating the charcoal category and resisting the onslaught of private label manufacturers. The bigger problem is that the overall category is shrinking, as consumers opt for the speed, convenience and safety of gas grills.

However, charcoal grills do have a strong perceived advantage over gas grills: better taste. To increase sales of Kingsford charcoal, I would recommend that the brand promotes the food flavor benefit to food aficionados, also known as foodies. The latest stats show that 54 percent of all American consumers identify as foodies. A potential positioning statement could be:

For foodies who want the best-tasting grilled food, Kingsford is grilling charcoal. Unlike gas grills, Kingsford charcoal contains natural elements such as pine, spruce and charred softwoods that provide a natural, unique flavor that will have you and your guests salivating for more.

In terms of the marketing plan, there are a couple of things I would recommend:

- *Distribution.* I would recommend selling Kingsford charcoal in high-end grocery stores known to foodies. Whole Foods and Trader Joe's come to mind. I would recommend in-store advertising and promotions that utilize the Kingsford positioning statement including:
  o *In-store signage*
  o *Stickers on meat, fish and vegetable products*
  o *Cooking demonstrations that utilize and prominently feature Kingsford products*
- *Product.* I would suggest launching new Kingsford SKUs that promote the consumer's belief that Kingsford charcoal produce better tasting food. One approach could be: manufacture charcoal infused with special flavors such as orange peel, lemon zest, sweet onion or hot peppers. Or create flavors that compliment certain types of meats such as steak, pork or fish.

And perhaps even invent charcoal flavors that are reminiscent of different cuisines such as Cajun or Korean charcoal.

- *Price.* With the new product SKUs that promote flavor, I believe we can raise the price of Kingsford charcoal from $8 to $10 a bag to perhaps $15 a bag. Consumers will be willing to pay more to have more exotic flavors.

- *Promotions.* To support a line extension, I would encourage an above-the-line campaign to target foodies and the flavor message. For TV ads, I would recommend advertising on the Food Network. For online ads, I would suggest Google AdWords along with placements on AllRecipes.com and Epicurious.com. For print ads, I would recommend advertising in *Bon Appétit* and *Food & Wine* magazine.

Scorecard

Overall Rating	Excellent
Marketing Aptitude	Excellent
Plan	Excellent
Communication Skills	Excellent
Composure	Excellent
Satisfying Conclusion	Excellent

Comments

Candidate asked relevant questions and quickly sized up the situation. The assessment of broader category and consumer trends was dead on, and the positioning statement was well done. The promotional and pricing tactics were reasonable.

The candidate recognized that this was a marketing problem and appropriately utilized the Big Picture framework in a declining sales question.

The recommendation for the line extension shouldn't be taken lightly. I would have preferred stronger reasoning and analysis before jumping into the specifics of the plan. However, the promotional and pricing tactics make sense, if they truly are trying to push a line extension.

Kit Kat sales declined year-over-year. Why is that, and what would you do to address it?

Screenshot @KitKat

INTERVIEWER: Kit Kat just launched a new advertising campaign. Year-over-year analysis indicates that advertising campaign achieved a three percent lift for the brand. The following Kit Kat SKUs were featured in the ad campaign:

- *Kit Kat Green Tea Flavor.* 12 mini bars. Each mini bar is two fingers.
- *Kit Kat King Size.* Single package with eight fingers.
- *Kit Kat Party Bag.* 40 mini bars. Each mini bar is two fingers.

CANDIDATE: Can you tell me more about the advertising campaign?

INTERVIEWER: It was televised to a national audience between 7 and 10 p.m. on weekdays. It occurred about one month before Halloween.

CANDIDATE: What message was conveyed?

INTERVIEWER: Standard Kit Kat messaging: ability to break it apart, the crunch sound and the fact that it's a reward for a long day. I don't have a video clip to show you, but here's an example of a regular Kit Kat ad.

JWT for Kit Kat

CANDIDATE: How about competitors' advertising?

INTERVIEWER: In the given time frame, competitors also promoted their candies with messages that were in-line with the standard positioning. For example, Snickers position statement centered on satisfying hunger cravings while M&M's positioning emphasized variety and collection.

One thing to note, Kit Kat outpaced the competition when it came to share of voice. They surprised everyone else by spending so much.

CANDIDATE: Does that explain the three percent lift?

INTERVIEWER: Yes.

CANDIDATE: But not all SKUs experienced a three percent lift.

INTERVIEWER: That's correct.

CANDIDATE: Let's investigate the individual SKUs. How did consumers react to each SKU?

INTERVIEWER: Kit Kat's focus group and survey data indicated that all SKUs were popular with consumers. King Size was perfect for either those with a big appetite or wanted to share with a friend. Party Bag was ideal for families or social occasions. And Green Tea flavor was a hit for those who sought novelty or just liked the green tea taste.

CANDIDATE: So can I assume consumer demand for all three SKUs were reasonably high? And can I assume that the packaging was attractive?

INTERVIEWER: Yes.

CANDIDATE: How about channel distribution? Where were the products sold?

INTERVIEWER: Here's some background information on distribution channels.

	Grocery	Drug and convenience	Mass merchandisers	Club stores
Green Tea		✓		
Party				✓
King Sized	✓	✓	✓	

CANDIDATE: Interestingly, party size is only sold in club stores. Has our relationship with club stores changed?

INTERVIEWER: Our only club store relationship is with Costco. This year, Costco launched a chocolate wafer product under its private label Kirkland brand.

CANDIDATE: How did the Kirkland chocolate wafer launch affect Kit Kat Party's shelf space in Costco?

INTERVIEWER: Last year, Costco prominently placed Kit Kat at the end of the aisle, which is also known as an end cap. However, with the introduction of the Kirkland chocolate wafer, they've replaced Kit Kat with Kirkland on the coveted end cap space.

CANDIDATE: And where is Kit Kat Jumbo?

INTERVIEWER: Costco put us in the back of the aisle.

CANDIDATE: Are our channel woes with Costco the reason for the poor sales?

INTERVIEWER: Yes.

CANDIDATE: Perfect, we found our culprit. Would you like me to make some recommendations on how we could address our Costco issues?

INTERVIEWER: Go for it.

CANDIDATE: Give me a moment to collect my thoughts.

Candidate takes 60 seconds

CANDIDATE: To address Kit Kat's shelf space issues with Costco, here are three ideas I have in mind:

1. *Give Costco co-op marketing dollars.* Pay Costco co-op marketing dollars to pay for the end cap space. Co-op marketing dollars could also be used to feature the Kit Kat party bag in Costco's publications, such as their coupon book.

2. *Offer to produce Costco's chocolate wafers.* If Costco is intent on offering a private label version of the chocolate wafer, Kit Kat could offer to manufacture, deliver and handle support for Kirkland's chocolate wafer brand. Kit Kat would cannibalize itself, but it's better than having a competitor steal share from Kit Kat.

3. *Pursue alternative distribution channels.* While Costco is a prominent club store player, it's not the only distribution channel available to Kit Kat. Kit Kat can pursue relationships with other club stores such as Sam's Club or BJ's. Kit Kat can even pursue non-club store retailers for the Party Bag, such as grocery and mass merchandisers.

Scorecard

Overall Rating	Excellent
Marketing Aptitude	Excellent
Plan	Excellent
Communication Skills	Excellent
Composure	Excellent
Satisfying Conclusion	Excellent

Comments

Candidate asked relevant questions to assess the situation and arrive at the true problem behind declining sales for the party bag: distribution woes. Candidate confidently came up with three suggestions on how to resolve the issue.

The candidate didn't use a fancy framework here. A note to framework-obsessed candidates: sometimes natural curiosity, logic and thought-out ideas are what it takes to impress the interviewer.

Colgate toothpaste sales are flat, but market share has gone down. What happened and how would you improve it?

INTERVIEWER: Colgate toothpaste's American annual sales were $1.5 billion for the past two years. Market share is down two percent compared to last year. You're responsible for explaining this situation and recommending a solution.

CANDIDATE: What's the annual growth rate for toothpaste sales?

INTERVIEWER: The industry grows at the same rate as GDP, which is three percent per year.

CANDIDATE: What's the market share Colgate and its competitors?

INTERVIEWER: There are two main competitors that we care about in the toothpaste category: Crest and Burt's Bees. Here's the market share data for Colgate and the others.

Toothpaste Unit Share for the Last Two Years

	Last Year	This Year
Crest	15%	15%

Colgate	14%	12%
Burt's Bees	1%	3%
Other	70%	70%

CANDIDATE: What is the average retail price for each player?

INTERVIEWER: Here's the average retail price for toothpaste in the last 12 months:

Average Retail Price for Toothpaste, Last 12 Months

	Average Retail Price
Crest	$3.75
Colgate	$3.25
Burt's Bees	$12.25
Other	$5.65

CANDIDATE: It looks like Burt's Bees is doing well. What explains its success despite being three times as expensive as the competition?

INTERVIEWER: They're growing strongly in the young families segment.

CANDIDATE: What is the young families segment, and what about Burt's Bees is appealing to them?

INTERVIEWER: Young families are defined as households with children less than 10 years old. The parents are concerned about product safety, so they find Burt's Bees appealing.

CANDIDATE: Is Burt's Bees' advertising and packaging explicitly promoting the safety benefit?

INTERVIEWER: No.

CANDIDATE: Are parents possibly inferring that Burt's Bees' is safe because it's made of natural and organic ingredients?

INTERVIEWER: Yes.

CANDIDATE: It's interesting that Colgate is suffering a year-over-year market share decline but Crest isn't it. Does Crest have an organic toothpaste line?

INTERVIEWER: No.

CANDIDATE: Are they affected? Or more precisely, is Crest losing sales due to consumer preference for natural, organic toothpaste?

INTERVIEWER: Yes.

CANDIDATE: Here are some possible reasons why they've been able to maintain market share, despite the consumer trend toward preferring natural, organic toothpaste. Crest is either:

- Discounting their current products
- Introducing and selling a new product
- Growing in a new customer segment

Is it any one of those reasons?

INTERVIEWER: Crest has launched a new toothpaste product in the last 12 months. It's an ultra-whitening product that they call internally, Ultra Ultra.

CANDIDATE: Has Ultra Ultra expanded the whitening category, stealing share from other whiteners, or none of the above?

INTERVIEWER: Before Ultra Ultra's launch, consumers who care about the whitening product benefit found whitening toothpastes available for purchase to be good enough. However, the large majority of the whitening segment is intrigued by Ultra Ultra's packaging and secret whitening agent. They are willing to pay a 20 percent premium for it.

CANDIDATE: Does Colgate have an ultra-whitening solution ready?

INTERVIEWER: Yes, once Ultra Ultra hit the market, Colgate rushed to develop an ultra-whitening product. But it won't be available for another two years.

CANDIDATE: Does Colgate have an organic line available?

INTERVIEWER: No, they completely fell asleep at the wheel on that trend, just like Crest.

CANDIDATE: Thanks for all the helpful information. Is there anything else you think might be helpful for me to know?

INTERVIEWER: No, I don't think I have any other important points to add.

CANDIDATE: Give me a moment to collect my thoughts and provide my recommendation.

Candidate takes 90 seconds.

CANDIDATE: The reason Colgate is losing market share while sales are flat is because of the organic toothpaste trend. Young families like the product benefit around safety, and they're not price sensitive.

By launching an ultra-whitening product, Crest has offset the growing trend toward organic and natural products. We believe that sales growth of their new ultra-whitening product will start tapering off.

The key question for Colgate: how does it get into the organic toothpaste market? Colgate can either develop an organic line or acquire an organic line. If it acquires an existing brand, Colgate would have a pre-existing customer base and a brand with awareness, interest and loyalty. It'll also minimize time-to-market delays.

If Colgate tries to build an organic brand, it'll take time to do so. The brand might not have the right production know-how or the distribution partnerships, especially with neighborhood and specialty stores such as Whole Foods. Furthermore, having Colgate develop a natural, organic brand may seem slightly inconsistent with consumer expectations. Any product branded as Colgate is likely to be perceived as mass produced and anything but natural.

Scorecard

Overall Rating	Excellent
Marketing Aptitude	Excellent
Plan	Excellent
Communication Skills	Excellent
Composure	Excellent
Satisfying Conclusion	Above Average

Comments

This is a declining sales question that tested a candidate to assess a new market opportunity, organic toothpaste. It also tested the candidate's judgment in whether they buy or build their way into the organic toothpaste market; many candidates will see the similarities with a merger and acquisitions case.

Generally, for new market opportunity we'd want to evaluate three different factors: profitability, strategic fit and operational capabilities. The candidate's answer didn't exactly touch on these points here, but I can't blame him. Consumer preferences are pointing so strongly toward organic products that it probably wouldn't have taken much evidence to convince most interviewers.

For the buy or build recommendation, the candidate outlines several solid arguments for acquiring an existing firm.

One area of improvement: I would have liked to see the candidate assess partnerships as a potential solution.

Chapter 6 Launching a New Product

Launching a new product can actually refer to three different types of case interview questions. The first type is the ""go or no-go": Should the company launch a new product? The second type is that while company has made a decision to launch a new product, there's a question about whether or not it should use an existing brand name for the new product. The third type is related to the second. That is, the decision to launch a new product has already been made, but what should the launch marketing plan be?

What is the Interviewer Looking For?

The interviewer's objective is different depending on which question-type it is. If the interviewer is asking you to make a "go or no-go" decision, they're judging your ability to construct an argument for why they should launch or not launch, using quantitative and qualitative reasons and evidence.

If the interviewer is asking you whether or not they should use an existing brand name on a new product, the interviewer is evaluating your branding knowledge and judgment.

If the interviewer is asking you to put together a launch plan, they're evaluating your ability to think strategically as well as your ability to come up with a tactical plan.

How to Approach the Questions

Should The Company Enter a New Market?

For this question, your answer should include both qualitative and qualitative analysis. Qualitative reasons for entering a market could include:

- *Gather insights.* Insights could include demand, preferences and operational know-how.
- *New markets.* A new venture could help tap into a new segment that's not part of the company's traditional audience.
- *Competitive response.* Entering a new market may be a way to deter or harm competition. Launching a new product could also cause a competitor to lose focus.

The quantitative portion should be centered on profitability of the initiative. A powerful yet simple tool to determine profitability is break-even analysis.

Break-even Analysis

Break-even analysis is helpful in determining the minimum number of units to not lose money in a new venture. Exaggerating for the sake of discussion, let's say the break-even point for Wal-Mart private label paper clips is 10 units sold.

Armed with this number, we can do a gut check and ask, "Is it likely that Wal-Mart will sell 10 paper clips?" With its brand, retail footprint and customer base, Wal-Mart can definitely sell 10 paper clips. After completing this gut-check we are confident that this is a worthwhile endeavor to pursue.

Here's the formula for break-even analysis:

Total Revenue = Total Cost

Total Revenue = Total Fixed Costs (FC) + Total Variable Costs (VC)

Price (P) x Quantity (Q) = FC + VC x Q

(P-VC) * Q = FC

Q = FC / (P – VC)

How Should the Company Launch a New Product?

If the interviewer's intent is to determine how you would launch a new product, your best bet is to use the Big Picture framework. It's appropriate for answering questions around marketing plans and tactics.

Should an Existing Brand Name Be Used on a New Product?

For questions around whether a new product should use an existing brand name, I'd suggest answering with the following criteria:

1. *Awareness.* Does the brand have strong awareness? Is it something that would stand out from lesser-known competitive brands?
2. *Favorability.* Does the brand have a positive, rather than a negative, perception?
3. *Fit.* Do the associations with existing brand fit with the new category?

Difference between Brand and Line Extensions

Many marketers use the terms brand extension and line extension interchangeably. However, they mean different things. A brand extensions is a new product that uses an existing brand name, but in a different category from the original brand.

For example, Virgin originally referred to a record shop brand. However, the company has extended the brand into new categories, unrelated to Virgin's record shop, including Virgin Mobile and Virgin America. Virgin Mobile is their wireless service while Virgin America is their United States-based airline.

They utilize the Virgin brand, but the brand extensions are completely unrelated. The first one is a smartphone while the latter is an airline.

As an aside, it's worth mentioning that there is a common theme between Virgin's unrelated businesses: a rebel spirit. Virgin's nonconformist attitude is largely derived from their founder: Richard Branson.

A line extension is a new product that uses an existing brand name, but in the same category as the original brand. For example, Coca-Cola is the original brand, and Diet Coke and Vanilla Coke are new products that share the same brand name and are in the same category.

Practice Questions

1. Should Nike start a dress shoe business?
2. Should General Mills use Yoplait or Pillsbury for their new frozen yogurt brand?
3. Should Microsoft use the Windows brand for its new watch?
4. How would you market a Thai drink in the United States?

Answers

Should Nike start a dress shoe business?

CANDIDATE: If you don't mind, I'd like to ask a couple clarifying questions.

INTERVIEWER: Go for it.

CANDIDATE: I'm assuming the goal of starting a dress shoe business is to increase profits. Is that correct?

INTERVIEWER: Why else do you think Nike would start a dress shoe business?

CANDIDATE: Off the top of my head, they could also start a dress shoe business because:

- *Learning.* Building a dress shoe business may lead to learning about manufacturing better shoes, marketing shoes more effectively or selling shoes in a different way. For instance, Starbucks owns a small group of independent coffee stores like Roy Street Coffee. Starbucks used it as an opportunity to test new product and retail concepts. The new Starbucks wine bars were inspired by a test concept at Starbucks' Roy Street Coffee store.
- *Customer access.* It's possible that dress shoe wearers aren't our typical target customer. By going to this business, we might access a new segment.
- *Competitive response.* Like military warfare, corporations can open new fronts to distract the enemy. Google executives once mentioned that they every time the then five-person Google Docs team released a new feature, thousands on the Microsoft Office team were scrambling to respond.

INTERVIEWER: Good ideas. There are no subtle strategic undertones here. Nike just wants to make more money.

CANDIDATE: Did you want me to explore this qualitatively, or were you looking for a profitability analysis?

INTERVIEWER: Focus on profits.

CANDIDATE: Give me a moment to get organized.

Candidate takes 60 seconds

CANDIDATE: Profitability is revenue minus costs. On the revenue side, it is price * quantity sold. On the cost side, it's fixed costs and variable costs.

Let's start by exploring revenue by starting with customer segments and estimating demand.

INTERVIEWER: Sounds like a plan.

CANDIDATE: Do you have any information about the customer segments?

INTERVIEWER: What do you think the customer segments could be in the dress shoe market?

CANDIDATE: Hmm, off the top of my head, I'd propose four segments:

- *"Just don't do it."* They don't have dress shoes. It's just not what they do.
- *Practical.* These are folks who only wear dress shoes because it's a job requirement. They don't want to spend too much on dress shoes. And it doesn't have to be trendy. As long as the dress shoe looks like it's in good shape, they're happy. Their average

dress shoe spend range is $50 to $100. They purchase once every 18 months.

- *Fashion-forward.* For these 20 to 30 year olds, looking fashionable is important. They don't have a lot of disposable income, but they will save or purchase on credit to get a pair of good shoes. Their average spend range is $100 to $300. They purchase shoes once every 9 months.

- *Prestige.* Folks in this segment have a median age of 58. They're executives working in traditional industries where formal dress is the norm. They spend $300 to $600 on a pair of shoes. They purchase shoes three times a year.

Let's estimate the annual purchases by segment:

Segment	Share	Size (millions)	Shoes purchased per year	Total purchases (millions)
Just don't do it	38%	60	0	0
Practical	40%	63	0.67	42
Fashion-forward	20%	32	1.33	42
Prestige	2%	3	3	9
Total		158		94

INTERVIEWER: Where did you get the segment share and size numbers?

CANDIDATE: I've assumed that segment share for "Just don't do it," Practical, Fashion-forward and Prestige to be 38, 40, 20 and 2 percent respectively.

For the segment size, I assumed we're focusing on the American market. I believe there are roughly 315 million people in the United States. We're catering to men, so that takes that number down to 158 million. From there, I just multiplied the segment shares with 158 million.

INTERVIEWER: Thanks for clarifying.

CANDIDATE: Now let's estimate the revenue by segment:

Segment	Total purchases (millions)	Range	Price midpoint	Total revenue (billions)
Just don't do it	0	$0	$0	0
Practical	42	$50-$100	$75	$3.2
Fashion-forward	42	$100-$300	$200	$8.4
Prestige	9	$300-$600	$450	$4.3
Total	94			$15.8

CANDIDATE: For the next step of the break-even analysis, can you tell me the costs?

INTERVIEWER: What would you like to know?

CANDIDATE: I'd like to understand the fixed costs and variable costs for this project.

INTERVIEWER: Here's the data that we have on variable and fixed costs. All values are in millions. There's no breakout on variable costs.

Segment	Practical	Fashion-forward	Prestige
R&D	$2	$4	$5
SG&A	$40	$70	$50
Other	$40	$40	$40
Total Fixed Costs	$82	$114	$95
Total Variable Costs	$15	$20	$25

CANDIDATE: If Nike decides to invest in one segment, are there cost savings if they enter a second and third segment?

INTERVIEWER: In real life, yes. But for the sake of discussion, let's assume no.

CANDIDATE: Give me a moment to complete my breakeven calculations.

118

INTERVIEWER: Okay.

Candidate writes the following:

Break-even Analysis

Total Revenue = Total Cost

Total Revenue = Total Fixed Costs (FC) + Total Variable Costs (VC)

Price (P) x Quantity (Q) = FC + VC x Q

(P-VC) * Q = FC

Q = FC / (P – VC)

Break-even for Practical Segment

Q = $82 million / ($75 - $15) = 1.4 million

Break-even for Fashion-Forward Segment

Q = $114 million / ($200 - $20) = 633 thousand

Break-even for Prestige Segment

Q = $95 million / ($450 - $25) = 224 thousand

CANDIDATE: To break-even, Nike would need to sell 1.4 million shoes in the practical segment, 633,000 shoes in the fashion-forward segment and 224,000 shoes in the prestige segment, respectively.

INTERVIEWER: Is this how much Nike sells the shoes to the channel?

CANDIDATE: Ah, you're right. I've been using the retail price. What discount does the channel get?

INTERVIEWER: Even though it's likely to be much higher, for the sake of discussion, let's say it's half off.

CANDIDATE: Okay, let me redo my calculations.

Candidate takes 40 seconds

INTERVIEWER: To break-even, Nike would have to sell 3.6 million shoes in the practical segment, 1 million shoes in the fashion-forward segment and 410,000 shoes in the prestige segment, respectively.

CANDIDATE: Doing a quick sanity check, here's the equivalent market share to achieve the break-even volume in year one:

Segment	Breakeven Volume	Total Volume	Equivalent Market Share
Practical	3,644,444	42,000,000	9%
Fashion-forward	1,025,000	42,000,000	2%
Prestige	410,000	9,000,000	5%

CANDIDATE: I'm getting close to a recommendation, but I have a few more questions.

INTERVIEWER: Go for it.

CANDIDATE: For each segment, what are the projected segment growth rates, and how strong is the competition in each segment?

Segment	Annual growth rate	Competition
Practical	2%	High
Fashion-forward	3%	Medium
Prestige	4%	Low

CANDIDATE: Great, let me jot down one more note.

Segment	Avg. To-Channel Price	COGS	Gross Margin
Practical	$37.50	$15	60%
Fashion-forward	$100	$20	80%
Prestige	$225	$25	89%

COGS = cost of goods sold

CANDIDATE: Here's my recommendation: from a strictly profitability point of view, I recommend that Nike enter the dress shoe market. The most attractive segments are fashion-forward and prestige. To break-even, Nike would only need 2 and 5 percent market share respectively. Given Nike's relationships with retail buyers and channel know-how, it seems reasonable to gain the market share necessary to be profitable. Furthermore, these two segments are less competitive, have higher gross margins and higher growth rates.

The practical segment is not recommended. It has low gross margins, high competition and a tepid growth rate. Most importantly, to break even, Nike would have to achieve 9 percent market share, in a fragmented industry where any a single competitor with market share between 10 and 20 percent is considered a market leader. This indicates that it would take more time for Nike to recoup its initial investment in the practical segment.

Scorecard

Overall Rating	Excellent
Marketing Aptitude	Excellent
Plan	Excellent
Communication Skills	Excellent
Composure	Excellent
Satisfying Conclusion	Excellent

Comments

Candidate did a good job with the response. The one area of improvement: the break-even analysis was strictly for the first year. I would have liked the candidate to factor in revenues and costs for several years into the future. As part of a multi-year analysis, the candidate should make some assumptions about annual growth. An astute candidate would also ask and if appropriate, factor in decrease in variable costs due to increased economies of scale.

Should General Mills use Yoplait or Pillsbury for their new frozen yogurt brand?

INTERVIEWER: General Mills decided to enter the frozen yogurt market. They're considering using the Yoplait or Pillsbury to co-brand the new venture. How would you evaluate this opportunity? Which brand would you leverage and why?

CANDIDATE: Just to clarify, are you asking me to evaluate and make a recommendation on whether General Mills should pursue the frozen yogurt opportunity? Or has the decision already been made, and are you asking me to recommend whether the yogurt should be branded as Yoplait or Pillsbury?

INTERVIEWER: The decision's been made. Assume that General Mills performed the due diligence and determined that they will pursue the opportunity. Your job is to recommend whether they should use the Yoplait or Pillsbury brand on the frozen yogurt.

CANDIDATE: Thanks for clarifying. When I think about how I evaluate whether a new product should leverage an existing brand, I think of three things:

- *Awareness*. Is the existing brand well known by the target audience?
- *Favorability*. Does the target audience think favorably of the existing brand?
- *Fit*. Are the brand associations of the existing brand in-line with what the new product would like be known for?

Before I evaluate this opportunity along these three dimensions, I'd like to get some background information. Can you give me more information about how General Mills plans to sell the frozen yogurt?

INTERVIEWER: General Mills has partnered with a prominent fast food chain to sell frozen yogurt. The name of the fast food chain is confidential.

CANDIDATE: Can you tell me more about the fast food chain's customers, and what they look for in a dessert and/or frozen yogurt?

INTERVIEWER: The fast food chain is a fast casual restaurant. This restaurant doesn't offer full table service, but promises higher quality food at a reasonable price.

Customers buy frozen yogurt because they like the taste, and they buy it to reward themselves. Frozen yogurt competes with ice cream. Yogurt fans prefer frozen yogurt because they consider it healthy. Frozen yogurt is made from milk not cream.

CANDIDATE: I know Yoplait is a yogurt brand, and Pillsbury is a baking brand. Can you tell me a little bit more about customer perception of each?

INTERVIEWER: You are correct. Pillsbury is a baking brand known for products that allow consumers to bake delicious treats. Pillsbury's products allow consumers to bake everything from biscuits, cakes and cookies. Pillsbury is perceived as convenient but not high quality. Consumers widely believe that to make fresh, delicious tasting baked goods you should cook from scratch.

Yoplait has a mixed past. Yogurt is generally known as a healthy product that's good for us. However, Yoplait has had some press in the last couple of years for having high-fructose corn syrup (HFCS). HFCS is an artificial sweetener that has been linked to America's rising diabetes and obesity trend. Under consumer pressure, Yoplait removed HFCS from its yogurt.

CANDIDATE: One last thing I forgot to ask, what are the aided awareness numbers for Pillsbury and Yoplait?

INTERVIEWER: What do you mean by aided awareness?

CANDIDATE: Percent of people that recognize Pillsbury and Yoplait, when shown a list of brand names.

INTERVIEWER: Pillsbury and Yoplait's aided awareness levels are 65 and 75 percent, respectively.

CANDIDATE: Thanks for all the information. Give me a couple seconds to collect my thoughts, and I'll be prepared to make my recommendation.

Candidate takes 90 seconds

CANDIDATE: General Mills has decided to enter the frozen yogurt market. The frozen yogurt will be distributed at an undisclosed fast food chain. General Mills has asked me to make a recommendation on whether or not they should use Pillsbury and Yoplait brands for this new product. When evaluating this decision, I laid out three criteria: awareness, favorability and fit. Here's how the two brands measure up to the criteria:

	Pillsbury	Yoplait
Awareness	⇧	⇧
Favorability	⇩	⇩
Fit	⇩	⇔
Overall	⇩	⇔

Let me review the table. Both Pillsbury and Yoplait have reasonable awareness that can help bring attention to the new frozen yogurt brand. Favorability of the brands is poor, especially considering that the frozen

124

yogurt will be sold at a restaurant known for high quality food. Pillsbury is primarily known for convenience, not high quality baked goods. Yoplait is associated as the market leader for yogurt. However, it's had a checkered past when it comes to using not-so-good ingredients such as HFCS.

Pillsbury's fit with frozen yogurt is not ideal. Pillsbury is a bakery brand, not dairy. Yoplait is a yogurt brand, so the fit is better. However, if I were to take a guess, I wouldn't automatically assume that a yogurt brand automatically conveys success as a frozen yogurt. Frozen yogurt and regular yogurt are different, not just in tastes, but in when they are eaten.

Given this, I would dismiss Pillsbury as a branding option. I would consider Yoplait. However, with its negative brand equity in the yogurt category, especially with the inferior products, that idea doesn't sit too well with me. Quite honestly, I would recommend that General Mills sell frozen yogurt under a completely new brand for three reasons. First, a new brand doesn't inherit any negative or awkward associations from existing brands. Second, since the General Mills frozen yogurt will be sold in the partner's restaurant, I imagine the frozen yogurt will be an exclusive. That is, there won't be competitive yogurts in the store. As a result, the clerks just need to convince the consumers on the category benefit, and they'll purchase. Lastly, the new frozen yogurt can leverage the associations from the restaurant, which is known for serving high-quality foods.

Scorecard

Overall Rating	Excellent
Marketing Aptitude	Excellent
Plan	Excellent

Communication Skills	Excellent
Composure	Excellent
Satisfying Conclusion	Excellent

Comments

Candidate offers a logical approach to the question. He shares his co-branding scorecard. He also asks good questions about the chain's customers, the target audience and why they buy frozen yogurt. It's a balanced assessment of co-branding options and the candidate gives a balanced argument on why they should have a new brand.

Should Microsoft use the Windows brand for its new watch?

INTERVIEWER: Microsoft is launching a new wristwatch that allows users to receive calls, emails and texts. It'll show weather information as well. Should Microsoft use the Windows brand for the new watch?

CANDIDATE: Do you mind if I take a moment to scratch out some thoughts?

INTERVIEWER: Okay.

Candidate takes 20 seconds

CANDIDATE: When I think about brand extensions, I keep three criteria in mind:

- *Awareness.* Is the brand we're leveraging well known to the target audience?
- *Favorability.* Does the brand have positive associations?
- *Fit.* Are the brand associations relevant?

INTERVIEWER: The Windows brand has high awareness. It's one of the most prevalent products on this Earth, so it probably has brand awareness of over 90 percent.

Unfortunately, the Windows brand is unlikely to be favorable. If you were to ask my friends, they'll identify Windows with being evil, traditional and outdated. It's also known to be unreliable, especially with the notorious blue screen of death.

Lastly, the Windows brand isn't a good fit. The Windows brand has a closer association to operating systems and software. Please tell me if I'm wrong, but Microsoft is selling the entire device, not just the operating system on the new watch. By calling it a Windows watch, it could give consumers a perception that Windows is only supplying the operating system, just like Microsoft only supplies the operating system for its Windows Phone devices. (Other companies, such as Nokia, HTC and Samsung provide the hardware devices for Windows Phone.)

Scorecard

Overall Rating	Excellent
Marketing Aptitude	Excellent
Plan	Excellent
Communication Skills	Excellent
Composure	Excellent
Satisfying Conclusion	Excellent

Comments

The response is nicely done. The candidate introduces the judging criteria, getting him and the interviewer on the same page. The criteria are reasonable, and he methodically reviews how a Windows brand would impact this brand extension.

How would you market a Thai drink in the United States?

INTERVIEWER: You are charged with marketing a drink called Dang Kabam. It's had mediocre sales in Thailand. What would you consider when bringing the product to the American market?

I'd like to learn a little bit more about the product. Do you mind if I ask some questions?

INTERVIEWER: Sure. What would you like to know?

What's in the drink?

INTERVIEWER: Packaged in an amber-colored medicine bottle, the most notable ingredients are taurine and caffeine. These two ingredients are known to improve alertness and mental performance.

Who uses it?

INTERVIEWER: Thai truck drivers and laborers are the primary consumers. Dang Kabam helps them cope with the long hours on the job. White collar professionals avoid the drink because of the blue collar perception. Others don't like the taste.

How much does it cost?

INTERVIEWER: In Thailand, it costs an equivalent of 50 American cents.

Thanks for the background information. Correct me if I'm wrong, are you asking me to discuss my go-to-market strategy for Dang Kabam in the United States?

INTERVIEWER: Yes, you can think of it that way.

CANDIDATE: Give me a moment to collect my thoughts.

CANDIDATE: Here's what I'd consider when creating a go-to-market strategy.

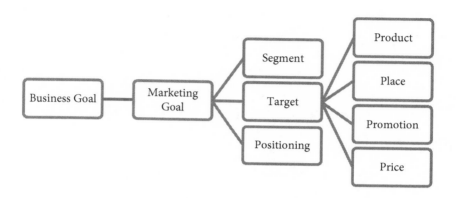

First step, I'd consider the business goal. We can choose to drive sales, maximize profits, or build market share. Since we're a new product, I'd recommend building market share. The quicker we can get the product in consumers' hands, the sooner they can promote the product to their friends.

INTERVIEWER: Sounds reasonable.

CANDIDATE: I'd also want to specify a timeframe for our marketing plan. Let's say it is one year.

Next, I'd like to talk about our marketing goal. Since this is a new market, we'll focus on acquisition. Also, this is a new product and brand, so we should focus our marketing plans on top-of-the-funnel activities: building awareness and interest.

INTERVIEWER: Okay.

CANDIDATE: For segmentation, we could do it along demographic, behavioral, attitudinal or aspirational lines. We could target truck drivers, like they did in Thailand, but I'd like to consider other segments.

There's one segment that I feel has a lot of potential: night clubbers. They appreciate the stimulant product benefit. They have a higher willingness to pay given the cost of a night out. And if Dang Kabam could be positioned as a mixer that's combined with other alcoholic beverages, it could get rid of that awful taste.

INTERVIEWER: I like your thoughts on the target segment. So what marketing tactics would you use?

CANDIDATE: Here are a couple of thoughts that I have:

- *Packaging.* Don't inherit the medicine bottle packaging that Dang Kabam used in Thailand. Instead, update the packaging with a more contemporary look more suitable for clubs.
- *Price.* Go for a premium price strategy. Given that coffee is often sold for $2 to $3 each, I'd raise Dang Kabam's price from $.50 to $3.
- *Distribution.* If we're targeting clubbers, naturally it makes sense to utilize clubs and bars as a distribution channel.
- *Promotions.* Increase awareness by doing above-the-line tactics such as TV, video and online.

Scorecard

Overall Rating	Excellent
Marketing Aptitude	Excellent
Plan	Excellent
Communication Skills	Excellent

Composure	Excellent
Satisfying Conclusion	Excellent

Comments

This question feels like a new market entry question, but it's not. The decision to enter the U.S. market has already been made. Your job as the candidate is to determine the go-to-market strategy. In other words, apply the Big Picture framework for developing marketing campaigns.

Chapter 7 Defending Against Competition

There will be a time for every brand when a competitor will challenge with a better product, aggressive advertising or identify new, untapped customers. There are countless brands that have lost sales to a more determined competitor. Defending against the competition is a natural part of any business; that's why this is a common interview question.

What Is the Interviewer Looking For?

For this interview question, the interviewer is evaluating the following:

- Does the candidate understand the company?
- Can the candidate diagnose how and why the competition is a threat to sales?
- Can the candidate come up with a creative plan that effectively counteracts the competitive threat?

How to Approach the Question

The first step is to assess the situation by asking questions:

- What is the competitive threat?
- Which customers are being targeted?
- How is the consumer responding to the competitor's moves?
- How is our brand affected by the situation?
- What is available in our arsenal to fight the threat?

The second step is to determine the goal of the competitive response. It could be general such as maintain or increase market share, or it could be specific, such as decrease call center cancellations from 80 percent to 60 percent.

The third step is to develop the plan. I would recommend using the Big Picture Framework. It'll make sure you hit all the elements of a thoughtful competitive marketing plan: which customer to target, how do we want to position the products and propose marketing tactics to address the competitive threat.

As a tip, here are some tactical responses that you can consider:

- Develop a loyalty program
- Improve product claims
- Reformulate the product
- Launch new line extensions
- Increasing advertising efforts

One of your key decisions is whether you'd respond to the competition directly. That depends on your market share. If the competitor is the market leader, you may want to call them out by name. That association helps smaller brands generate awareness, helping more consumers understand that you belong to a certain category.

However, if you are the market leader, you want to avoid calling out the competition. Here, the inverse will happen. You will inadvertently draw more attention to the competition, creating brand awareness among your customers around an unfamiliar brand.

Practice Question

1. As the brand manager for OxiClean Stain Fighter, how would you respond to Tide's new stain fighter product, Tide Boost?

Answer

As the brand manager for OxiClean Stain Fighter, how would you respond to Tide's new stain fighter product, Tide Boost?

CANDIDATE: I know OxiClean is your line of household detergents. However, I personally do not use the stain fighter category. Can you tell me more about it?

INTERVIEWER: The stain fighter category is an additive that helps remove laundry stains. It's applied in addition to your laundry detergent. It's also known as an in-wash booster.

CANDIDATE: Can you tell me more about the customers in the category?

INTERVIEWER: Moms, who deal with everything from grass stains to art-related accidents, are our most numerous customers. We recently ran a survey, and here's what category customers report as reasons why they chose a particular stain fighter brand:

- Gets stains out (85%)
- Makes clothes brighter (65%)
- Value (54%)
- Convenient and no mess (24%)
- Environmentally friendly (13%)

CANDIDATE: Can you tell me more about Tide Boost, and how it differs from OxiClean Stain Fighter?

INTERVIEWER: Tide Boost's motto is "Stains Out. No Doubt." OxiClean's current value proposition is "Cleaner, Whiter, Brighter."

Here's some data on how Boost's product SKUs match up with Stain Fighter's:

134

	Powder	Liquid	Spray	Gel	Pack
Stain Fighter	✓	✓	✓		
Boost	✓			✓	✓

CANDIDATE: What's OxiClean's market share relative to the competition?

INTERVIEWER: Here's the latest data from Nielsen's scanning database:

Stain Fighters Market Share in Last 12 Months

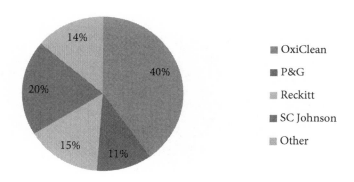

Rise Above the Noise

CANDIDATE: Do consumers like the gel and pack formats?

INTERVIEWER: Consumers find gel and pack to be less messy than powder and liquid formats.

CANDIDATE: What are the differences in price?

INTERVIEWER: We don't have detailed pricing information. But let's say that Tide is a premium brand while OxiClean is positioned as a value brand. Premium brands typically cost 50 percent more than value brands.

CANDIDATE: How are value brands perceived by consumers?

INTERVIEWER: I don't have consumer perception data, but you might infer consumer popularity based on segment growth rates. We classify consumers into four price segments: extreme value, value, mid and premium.

Segment	5 Year Growth
Extreme Value	11.7%
Value	1.5%
Mid	-10.1%
Premium	-17.4%

CANDIDATE: It looks like the more value-conscious segments are growing fastest. How are our advertising efforts?

INTERVIEWER: We're currently spending $20 million on above-the-line advertising. We're expecting Tide to spend $50 million to support the new brand.

CANDIDATE: How about distribution?

INTERVIEWER: Let's leave distribution out of the discussion. Assume that Stain Fighter and Boost's distribution capabilities are similar.

CANDIDATE: I think I have enough background data to craft my recommendation. Just to confirm our goal, I imagine the objective is to preserve market share?

INTERVIEWER: Yes, we want to maintain our 40 percent market share.

CANDIDATE: Do I have any budget limits?

INTERVIEWER: No, the sky is the limit.

CANDIDATE: Give me a moment to collect my thoughts and issue my final recommendation.

Candidate takes 45 seconds

CANDIDATE: To recap, OxiClean is a stain fighter that's needs to respond to a new product in the category, Tide Boost. OxiClean is the market leader with 40% market share, and the goal of our marketing efforts is to maintain and maybe increase market share. Given our market share lead, I would focus our marketing efforts on retaining our existing customers. Here are the top tactics I'd recommend to do so:

- *Stick with the "value" target segment.* The "value" and "extreme value" segments continue to grow. This is consistent with broader consumer trends of tighter budgets and being value conscious.
- *Modify product positioning.* The "cleaner, whiter" positioning is compelling, but doesn't hit directly at the category benefit: removing stains. I'd recommend product claims that revolve around "getting tough stains out," "breaking down stains," and "seek out stains."
- *Reformulate product.* Offer a new formula to give consumers a reason to believe the new product claims.
- *Fill gaps in the product portfolio.* Offer the gel and pack formats that are missing in OxiClean's lineup. Don't give current customers a chance to migrate to a competitor because the product format is not correct.
- *Co-branding opportunities.* Co-brand sibling products such as Arm & Hammer detergent and carpet odor eliminator with OxiClean. It'll help drive more awareness to OxiClean and reinforce OxiClean's brand with stain fighting.
- *Increase advertising.* Boost above-the-line advertising spend to match Tide's $50 million spend to maintain top-of-mind

awareness, positioning and perceived leadership in the category.

Scorecard

Overall Rating	Excellent
Marketing Aptitude	Excellent
Plan	Excellent
Communication Skills	Excellent
Composure	Excellent
Satisfying Conclusion	Excellent

Comments

The candidate led an in-depth discussion around the impending competitive threat, and he offered a detailed and logical plan to protect market share.

Some readers may be surprised how detailed and informed his recommendation is. Realize that the response's depth was only possible by taking the time upfront by asking good questions about the category, customer and competition.

Chapter 8 Competing against Private Label

For many consumer packaged goods companies, private label competition is one of their biggest threats to their business. From 2000 to 2010, private-label products gained nearly all of the growth in packaged food, beauty, personal care and home care categories. Private label goods have stolen share in almost all categories, and the volume has been staggering. For example, Kroger's private-label products account for 35 percent of the chain's total grocery units sold and 27 percent of its total revenue.

Private label is growing for the following reasons:

- *Consumer trends.* Consumers are getting more comfortable purchasing private-label goods. For instance, Bain & Company reports that in 2008, more than 90 percent have tried private labeled goods. It is an astonishing increase given than only 56 percent have tried private labels in 2004. Consumers increasingly view private label products as high quality, shedding their low quality perception from the 1980s.
- *Margins.* Private label goods have margins that are 10 percent better than their branded counterparts.
- *Differentiation.* Private label goods help differentiate from other retailers, who do not carry the same private label products.
- *Marketing efficiency.* Manufacturers spend 10 to 40 percent of their sales toward marketing. But for private label brands, the number is usually less than 2 percent.
- *Negotiation leverage.* Private label goods increase competition for a retailer's shelf space, increasing the rent retailers charge manufacturers for shelf space.

What is the Interviewer Looking For?

The interviewer is looking for a sound approach to competing against private label. That is, does the candidate identify relevant issues? Does the candidate have a reasonable plan to counter the private label threat? And are the tactics consistent with overall business objectives?

How to Approach the Question

When answering this question, keep in mind the range of potential responses below:

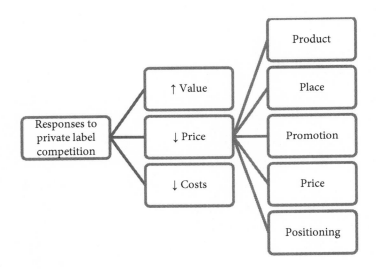

Increase Value

Manufacturers can increase value, either real or perceived, by introducing new products that either meet the needs of a new segment or more deeply meet the needs of an existing segment.

- *Launch new products for new, underserved segments.* Example: Tylenol didn't explicitly target children until they unveiled Children's Tylenol. It stunted private label's growth, especially in the children's market.

- *Launch new products for existing segments.* Example: In 1989, Gillette launched the Sensor razor. It cost nearly 10 times more than a private label razor, which sold for 40 cents. Gillette Sensor's marketing team convinced that it could serve its customers' needs more deeply with more innovative razors.

Decrease Price

Some brands may explicitly cut price in response to a new private label product. But there are ways to cut price in a more subtle fashion that's less damaging to brand names:

Manufacture private-label products

Kimberley-Clark manufactures private-label diapers for Costco under Costco's Kirkland brand. This improves Kimberley-Clark's economies of scale and asset utilization.

Kimberley-Clark also gained a competitive advantage. Kimberley-Clark accepted Costco's offer to remove Procter & Gamble's Pampers brand from its store shelves if Kimberley-Clark would provide customer support for Kirkland diapers.

Establish a fighting brand

A fighting brand is a bargain offering that's meant to compete with lower-priced competitors. A fighting brand has actual or perceived performance that's lower than the company's premium brand. For example, 3M's Post-It Notes brand sells for $25.13 while 3M's Highland brand sells for $9.90. Highland is manufactured with lower-quality adhesive.

Decrease Costs

Another way to compete with private label brands is to decrease costs. Decreasing costs could improve profit margins, compensating for decreased sales and possibly giving manufacturers increased flexibility to reduce price.

Manufacturers might want to try negotiating discounts with its suppliers, automating processes to reduce labor overhead, or simplify packaging to reduce COGS.

Practice Question

1. How would Aveeno compete with Costco's new body lotion?

Answer

How would Aveeno compete with Costco's new body lotion?

INTERVIEWER: Let's say Costco is about to launch a new body lotion. Can you list the three best ways Aveeno could respond?

CANDIDATE: Can I ask some clarifying questions?

INTERVIEWER: I apologize, but we're short on time. What are the three ways we could respond?

CANDIDATE: Hmm, let me see…

Candidate pauses for ten seconds

CANDIDATE: Here are three ways we could respond:

- Increase value
- Cut price
- Cut costs

We can make our product more compelling by increasing its value. We can offer more lotion for the same price or create a better product.

We can decrease price, reducing consumer's incentive to switch to a private label brand.

Lastly, we can cut costs. By increasing operational efficiency, it'll give us more flexibility to cut price, innovate better products, or protect ourselves from decreased sales.

INTERVIEWER: Thank you.

Scorecard

Overall Rating	Above Average
Marketing Aptitude	Above Average
Plan	Above Average
Communication Skills	Above Average
Composure	Excellent
Satisfying Conclusion	Above Average

Comments

This is considered just an above average response because it is not as developed as other responses we've seen. Unfortunately, the interviewer insisted on a quick answer, so there was no opportunity for the candidate to get information to provide a more convincing response.

The candidate made the most of an awkward situation and submitted a well-organized answer given the time limit.

Chapter 9 Critiquing a Marketing Effort

A common marketing interview question is, "Can you tell me a product that's marketed well?" I call this category of questions "Critiquing marketing efforts." This question can be dangerous if not handled with care.

What is the Interviewer Looking For?

This is a popular question because it's a casual, conversation question that can reveal a candidate's marketing enthusiasm and expertise. A talented marketer will likely jump into this question with gusto, offering copious details punctuated with excitement.

Less talented marketers will pose a perplexed look, tip toeing with trepidation.

How to Approach the Question

The question prompt is broad and vague, making this question hard. A good first step is to clarify what is meant by "product, marketed well." Perhaps the interviewer is narrowly asking for a product with a good ad campaign. Or maybe the interviewer is asking for a product with a well-formed marketing plan, which includes all the elements of a Big Picture framework.

Once you've clarified the question, approach the problem with a clear scorecard in mind. Tell the interviewer the scorecard in advance, so that you and the interviewer are evaluating your response with the same criteria.

I recommend that your criteria be related to the marketing fundamentals, whether it's STP, the 4P's or the value proposition. You need not have the same criteria each time you answer this question, as long as the thinking and judgment is sound.

Tip: What's an Ideal Product for This Question?

The best answers select products that are so bad or undifferentiated that it's commercial success must be clever marketing.

What if you can't think of a bad product off the top of your head? Think about a premium product that's a commodity. Here are some of my favorite examples:

- $3 Fiji water
- $36 Phiten titanium necklace
- $10,000 Chanel handbag

Not every marketer can sell water for $3 or a Chanel handbag for $10,000. It must be the marketing.

Practice Questions

1. Tell me about a terrible product that's marketed well.
2. Why is the iPod shuffle a terrible product marketed well?

Answers

Tell me about a terrible product that's marketed well.

CANDIDATE: The Snuggie. It looks ugly, but they sold millions.

Uncomfortable 3 second pause

INTERVIEWER: That's all you have to share?

CANDIDATE: Yes.

INTEVIEWER: I was expecting a little more.

CANDIDATE: Sorry, do you mind if I try again?

INTERVIEWER: Sure.

CANDIDATE: Thanks. The Snuggie is not a sophisticated product. As the packaging explains, it's a fleece blanket with sleeves.

The genius behind Snuggie's marketing is identifying an untapped customer scenario: people get cold when they're sitting on their favorite sofa or chair. Most people like to wrap themselves with a blanket. However, the problem with a blanket is that they can't use it hands-free. If they reach for a book, a TV remote or laptop, a regular blanket will slip down. By creating a blanket with sleeves, Snuggie customers can use their hands while keeping warm under your blanket.

The packaging doesn't look fancy, but it's remarkably effective. First, it explains what a Snuggie is, "The Blanket That Has Sleeves." Second, it explains the benefit customers will receive, "Keeps You Warm and Your Hands Free!" Lastly, the product box photos help customers imagine how they might use the product: watching TV, reading on the plane and working on the laptop from the sofa.

The Snuggie is priced right at $19.95. Why? It's an impulse purchase that many would consider purchasing for friends and family. Industry pundits believe the wholesale cost of the Snuggie is $5, creating tremendous incentive for retailers to feature in prominent locations, especially in an environment where the typical markup is 100 percent, not 300 percent.

Lastly, the Snuggie is a perfect gift for the winter holidays. Who doesn't want to stay warm?

Comments

Overall Rating	Above Average
Marketing Aptitude	Excellent, after the restart
Plan	Poor
Communication Skills	Excellent, after the restart
Composure	Excellent, after the restart
Satisfying Conclusion	Excellent, after the restart

Comments

This example shows how the initial one-line response is unsatisfying; it doesn't demonstrate the depth of a candidate's marketing insight.

I would rarely recommend that candidates apologize and restart. It's much better to get it perfect the first time. However, if the first attempt is a disaster, apologize, try again and hope that the interviewer is impressed by the second attempt.

Fortunately, the candidate's second attempt is a stellar response. It clearly calls out Snuggies' effective customer targeting, on-the-mark positioning and potent pricing.

Why is the iPod shuffle a terrible product marketed well?

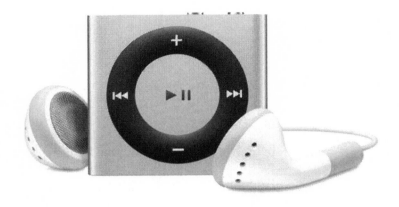

Screenshot / iPod shuffle

CANDIDATE: The iPod shuffle is a terrible product, but it's marketed well. Imagine selling an MP3 player that doesn't allow you to choose which song to play. Most people would consider that broken. That's the iPod shuffle, which Apple sold successfully for many years.

Rather than run away from the product's flaws, Apple marketing team embraced iPod shuffle's "random only" playback. Apple created an advertising campaign with the "Life is Random" tagline (TV ad: http://bit.ly/dVLVop). The commercial paired dancing silhouettes with a lively, upbeat soundtrack. The ad made it clear: If you aspire for a fun and exciting life, this product was made for you.

The iPod shuffle was introduced in 2005. About nine years later, the iPod shuffle maintains its premium pricing of $49. This is more remarkable when competitive products struggle to sell for more than $10, 20 percent of the iPod shuffle's price.

Scorecard

Overall Rating	Excellent
Marketing Aptitude	Excellent
Plan	Excellent
Communication Skills	Excellent
Composure	Excellent
Satisfying Conclusion	Excellent

Comments

It explains why it's a terrible product: "MP3 player that doesn't allow you to choose which song to play." It then explains how it took this "random only" feature and convert it into a memorable, aspirational marketing campaign.

Chapter 10 Critiquing Advertising

As a brand or marketing manager, a critical part of your role is to lead or manage the creation of marketing collateral, whether it's a brochure, product packaging, or an advertising campaign. During the marketing interview, it's common for the interviewer to ask you to critique a recent advertising campaign.

What is the Interviewer Looking For?

The interviewer wants to see that you can provide meaningful feedback on advertising creative, whether it's an in-house creative team or a third party ad agency.

How to Approach the Question

Use a scorecard when evaluating ad creative. I've got two ad critique scorecards that I'd recommend: MOB Method™ and ADPLAN.

MOB Method™

There are three parts to the MOB Method™:

M emorable

O bvious product

B enefit

I invented the method to critique Super Bowl TV ads. To help you remember, remember that a mob of players pounce on the football, and MOB will help you pounce and dissect Super Bowl (and regular) ads. MOB has three main parts.

Memorable

The ad has to grab attention. The viewer is making a choice of whether they're going to stick around or grab a beer. And if they've stuck around, is the ad memorable enough for them to think, discuss and tweet with their friends?

Obvious Product

Creative types tend to produce tear-jerking, Oscar-worthy ads. TV ads aren't meant to win the Sundance Film Festival. The point of an ad is to pitch products. It has to provide the viewer an idea of what's being promoted as well as a clear brand association.

I see a huge problem with this when I watch tablet commercials. All of them feel similar: inspirational soundtrack and images of a person using a tablet – filled with hope and potential. Heck, how would I know if it's promoting an iPad, a Nexus, a Galaxy Tab, or Kindle Fire? Commercials that don't clarify what's been promoted won't drive sales.

Benefit

Lastly, the ad has to explain the product benefit and produce evidence why they can back up that claim. It's not enough to say that you've got an ad for Coca-Cola, Camry, or Charmin. An ad should tell consumers why they should choose their brand over the competition.

Take Volvo for example. You buy a Volvo because their cars are safer than others. They invented the seat belt and reinforce their car with the strongest steel possible. If you're in the market for a safe, family car, it's Volvo all the way.

ADPLAN Framework

If you're looking for a framework that's more comprehensive, I'd recommend using ADPLAN. The ADPLAN framework was invented by Tim Calkins, a professor of marketing at Northwestern University's Kellogg School of Management.

A ttention

D istinction

P ositioning

L inkage

A mplification

N et Equity

The following table explains each criterion, along with an ad that exemplifies the criteria.

	Criteria Description	Example
Attention	Does the ad capture the consumer's attention?	Budweiser's *Whassup?* commercials from 1999 to 2002 caught viewer's attention for slurring the words "What's up?"
Distinction	Is the ad distinct from its competitors?	Whether it is trucks or tablets, numerous ad commercials are less than memorable because they use similar creative imagery and positioning as their competition.
Positioning	Is the positioning clear?	Altoids ads indicate that consumers who desire fresh breath should buy their "curiously strong mints."
Linkage	Is there a clear link between the advertisement and the company's brand or products?	A 2014 Budweiser Super Bowl ad tells a touching friendship story between a puppy and a Clydesdale. However, it's not clear how the company's beers relate to the ad.
Amplification	How does the consumer think about the ad afterward?	Soda Pop Board of America's ads promoting soda with young kids produced a negative impression with viewers, creating negative press long after the original ad was published.
Net equity	Is the advertisement consistent with the brand's cumulative	In the 2014 Super Bowl, Subway promoted a new sandwich topped with Fritos corn chips. At 580

history?	calories, this new sandwich (and ad) contradicts Subway's positioning over the last ten years: fresh and healthy food.

Practice Questions

1. Give me an example of an effective ad.
2. Give me an example of an ineffective ad.
3. Evaluate this print ad. Who is the target customer? What insights does it leverage? And what is the key message?
4. Give me an example of an effective Twitter campaign.
5. Give me an example of an effective brand post on Facebook.
6.

Overall Rating	Excellent
Marketing Aptitude	Excellent
Plan	Excellent
Communication Skills	Excellent
Composure	Excellent
Satisfying Conclusion	Excellent

Comments

Candidate chose a unique and memorable example. Tide's creative execution is stellar and bursting with color. The candidate's analysis was very detailed and on point. Bravo.

7. Give me an example of an effective brand post on Pinterest.
8. Give me an example of an effective brand post on Instagram.
9. When you walk down the supermarket aisle, what product jumps out and says "buy me" and why?
10. Give me an example of an innovative product package.

Answers

Give me an example of an effective ad.

CANDIDATE: One of my favorite ad campaigns comes from Aspirina, Bayer's aspirin brand in Brazil. They have two SKUs. One is regular aspirin. The other one is aspirin with caffeine, which is a stimulant.

Before I evaluate the ad, here's what I consider to be a memorable ad:

- Is it memorable?
- Does it clearly identify the product?
- Does it convey the product benefit?

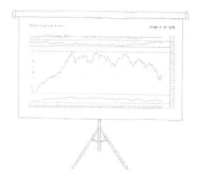

Image AlmapBBDO

Bayer also incorporated the same theme for another creative execution.

Here, the visual shows a slide presentation showing the annual financial report. There's reason to be pessimistic given the recent decline after a long plateau period.

The creative execution meets my first two criteria; it's memorable and clearly identifies the product.

It also meets my third criteria in that it conveys the product benefit, using a clever red-green color scheme. That is, the green product, regular aspirin, will get you through painful moments. But the red product, will keep you awake through the remaining 275 slides in the presentation.

Scorecard

Overall Rating	Excellent
Marketing Aptitude	Excellent
Plan	Excellent
Communication Skills	Excellent
Composure	Excellent
Satisfying Conclusion	Excellent

Comments

There's a good conversational tone here that isn't mechanical. It takes advantage of the MOB Method™.

Note that the candidate orients the listener by describing the ad first, before jumping into the analysis.

Give me an example of an ineffective ad.

Image Grey, Singapore

CANDIDATE: Here's an ineffective ad from Duracell. On the one hand, the creative execution is memorable. It's a haunting illustration that triggers a childhood emotion of toys coming to life. The Duracell product and logo on the right hand side makes clear identification of what it's promoting. And the tagline clarifies the product benefit that we can infer from the illustration: Our batteries last much longer than expected.

Screenshot / Energizer Bunny

But here's the main problem with the ad: Duracell's competition, Energizer has a stronger brand association of having long-lasting batteries, using the ever-ubiquitous Energizer bunny toy to reinforce that message, with the tagline, "The Energizer bunny keeps going and going and going."

Although the creative execution might be different, Duracell's copying of Energizer's value prop and a toy metaphor to convey this will lead to many consumers to have difficulty recalling the company behind this beautiful creative illustration. Many customers will assume that this is an Energizer, not Duracell ad. As a result, this advertisement is not effective because it inadvertently drives consumers to purchase a competitive product.

Scorecard

Overall Rating	Excellent
Marketing Aptitude	Excellent
Plan	Excellent
Communication Skills	Excellent
Composure	Excellent
Satisfying Conclusion	Excellent

Comments

The candidate analyzed the ad well. He immediately explained what the good points were, led the audience to its natural conclusion and ended with why it was ineffective, as claimed. The candidate's thought process was clear throughout the answer.

Evaluate this print ad. Who is the target customer? What insights does it leverage? And what is the key message?

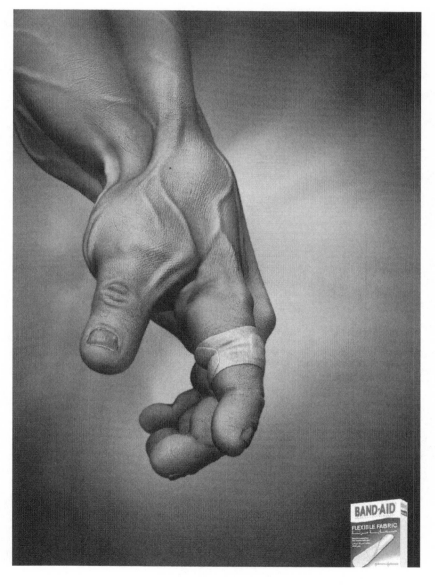

JWT Dubai

INTERVIEWER: Here's a print ad from Band-Aid. It shows a picture of the superhero, Incredible Hulk, with a Band-Aid wrapped around his finger. Who is the target customer, and what insights does it leverage?

CANDIDATE: The target customers are those who don't use bandages. This ad campaign leverages a unique insight: many people who suffer a small cut or prick believe that they don't need a bandage.

INTERVIEWER: So, what is the key message?

CANDIDATE: The key message is that even superheroes need bandages when they get hurt.

INTERVIEWER: Isn't the key message that Band-Aid's bandages are flexible, even for superheroes whose superpower is growing twice their normal size?

CANDIDATE: Let me take another look at the ad.

Candidate pauses briefly

CANDIDATE: Now that you mention it, I can see that message. It's been a while since I've watched the Incredible Hulk. But now that I think about it, Dr. Bruce Banner increases in size whenever he's angry. So I imagine what this ad is saying is the bandage is so flexible that it stays on, even when Dr. Banner grows in size to be the Incredible Hulk. It makes sense now why it says "Flexible Fabric" in tiny print in the lower right hand corner.

INTERVIEWER: Do you think this advertisement is aimed at existing customers?

CANDIDATE: The ad emphasizes the product benefit of "flexibility." This benefit message could be targeted to either current customers, to reinforce why they purchase Band-Aid, or new customers to help them choose between Band-Aid and its competition.

162

Scorecard

Overall Rating	Average
Marketing Aptitude	Below Average
Plan	Below Average
Communication Skills	Above Average
Composure	Excellent
Satisfying Conclusion	Above Average

Comments

This candidate had a rough start by not seeing the correct ad strategy and audience. However, once the interviewer corrected them, he got back on track and arrived with the appropriate answer. By admitting that he was incorrect, the candidate demonstrates maturity, with poise.

That error aside, the candidate's communication, thought process and conclusion was very strong.

It's not ideal to get it wrong in the first place, but it's worse to neglect the feedback and react poorly to criticism.

Give me an example of an effective Twitter campaign.

Screenshot / @Oreo

CANDIDATE: My favorite social media campaign was Oreo's tweet during the 2013 Super Bowl. At the Super Bowl, the lights went out for 20 minutes, and Oreo took full advantage of the opportunity by tweeting, "Power Out? No Problem. You can still dunk in the dark." It was accompanied by a large, gorgeous graphic.

Here's why I liked it: It was timely and relevant. It also reinforced a key product message: Oreo cookies are good for all occasions. And it also imparted a more subtle message: Oreo is the cookie brand that's fun, playful and bubbling with personality.

Finally, their response was very distinctive and memorable. Compare it to Audi's response below. (@MBUSA refers to Mercedes-Benz's Twitter account, their competitor.) Audi gets credit for a witty response to the lights out at the Super Bowl. However, it lacked Oreo's visual appeal.

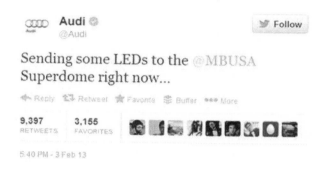

Screenshot / @Audi

Scorecard

Overall Rating	Above Average
Marketing Aptitude	Above Average
Plan	Above Average
Communication Skills	Average
Composure	Above Average
Satisfying Conclusion	Average

Comments

The candidate appears to be knowledgeable about social media marketing. However, his analysis comes across as formulaic and dry, especially with the usage of "first, second and finally" series.

The Audi comparison was confusing. The candidate compared two different brands and products. I understand that the candidate wanted to contrast two companies' responses during the same event: the Super Bowl, but it was an abrupt transition.

All-in-all, the candidate's intent is good, but it shows how important it is for candidates to stop, think and organize their thoughts before speaking. Otherwise, the answer will lack the desired impact.

Give me an example of an effective brand post on Facebook.

Tide
January 11 ☼

What's your 2014 wash style?

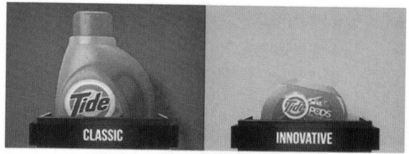

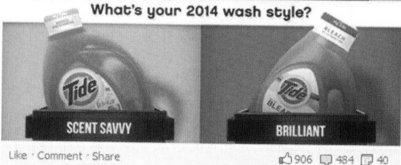

Like · Comment · Share   👍906 💬484 🔁40

Screenshot / @Tide

CANDIDATE: When I think about what makes an effective brand post on Facebook, here's what I consider:

1. Is it clear what's being advertised?
2. Is there a stunning photo?
3. Is the caption text too long?
4. Does it engage the user in a purposeful way?
5. Does it deliver a clear message?

Let's review how Tide's post stacks up against this criterion:

- *Brand identification.* The photo makes it clear that it's advertising Tide.
- *Photo quality.* The photo is sharp and colorful. I can easily read the text, and I can tell that it is promoting the same brand even though the packaging is different.
- *Brevity.* The reader isn't overwhelmed by text. Aside from the photo, it's a simple question, "What's your 2014 wash style?"
- *Engagement.* We can tell from the 484 comments that the call-to-action question worked. Tide got the users to interact in a dialogue with the community.
- *Message clarity.* The post makes it clear that there's a Tide for all wash occasions whether you're trying to get your clothes to smell good, shine brightly and so forth.

Tide did a fantastic job; it's one of the best brand posts I've seen on Facebook.

Scorecard

Overall Rating	Excellent
Marketing Aptitude	Excellent
Plan	Excellent
Communication Skills	Excellent
Composure	Excellent
Satisfying Conclusion	Excellent

Comments

Candidate chose a unique and memorable example. Tide's creative execution is stellar and bursting with color. The candidate's analysis was very detailed and on point. Bravo.

Give me an example of an effective brand post on Pinterest.

 from kate spade

Crunch Bunch 2 piece Feeding Set

the sweetest baby shower gift—the crunch bunch 2-piece feeding set, by kate spade new york (february 2014)

357 88 2

CANDIDATE: Kate Spade is one of the most effective brand advertisers on Pinterest. There are a couple of reasons why. As you can see from the picture, their products are always unique and eye-catching. The caption clearly explains what you're looking at and when it was released. It also succinctly indicates that it's perfect as a "baby shower gift." Lastly, the image aptly links to the purchase page. Pinterest is known to drive purchases. Shopify indicates that a customer from Pinterest has an average order size of $80, which is twice as large as an order from a Facebook user at $40.

Scorecard

Overall Rating	Average
Marketing Aptitude	Average
Plan	Average
Communication Skills	Above Average
Composure	Above Average
Satisfying Conclusion	Average

Comments

While the answer feels solid, the chosen example doesn't resonate with most interviewers.

Looking at the visual, it resembles a product details entry on an e-commerce web site: image, product description and a link to purchase.

The candidate would have better served to choose an example that resembled the community spirit of the new social media platforms. That is, something that's more conversational and authentic. This example feels a little too commercial; its intent to drive purchase feels a bit pushy.

By contrast, Lauren Conrad is a brand that uses Pinterest in a non-commercial way.

Conrad, a reality TV star turned fashion entrepreneur, pins clothes and accessories from the same websites her fans frequent. That doesn't mean her board doesn't feature clothes from her own fashion line.

170

Conrad pins content that is consistent with the spirit of the Pinterest community: Conrad supplements Pins with helpful articles (e.g. "5 Things to Try This Month") and uses the same breezy writing style as her fans.

5 Things to Try This Month
LaurenConrad.com

Screenshot / @LaurenConrad1

Give me an example of an effective brand post on Instagram.

CANDIDATE: Sharpie is my favorite brand on Instagram. Here's a recent post: they shared a hand drawn panda picture. A black Sharpie is placed on top of it. And the caption reads, "#FACT: You only need one #sharpie to draw a #panda."

Here are the reasons why I like it:

- It's an adorable, eye-catching visual.
- The brand association is clear from the picture.
- The unembellished visual reflects the spirit of the Instagram community: user-generated content.
- The caption is a meaningful reminder that beautiful creativity doesn't require sophisticated tools.

There is one thing that detracts from Sharpie's post: unnecessary hashtags. Do a quick search for: #FACT and #PANDA, and you'll find a lot of Instagram photos unrelated to Sharpie. If Sharpie could have a do over, I'd recommend choosing unique hashtags and possibly dispensing from using hashtags completely.

Scorecard

Overall Rating	Excellent
Marketing Aptitude	Excellent
Plan	Excellent
Communication Skills	Excellent
Composure	Excellent
Satisfying Conclusion	Excellent

Comments

The candidate nailed it. Most candidates would have chosen a famous brand such as Starbucks, Nike, H&M or Red Bull. Sharpie is an uncommon choice which grabs the interviewer's attention. The reasons for why it's a good Instagram post are clear and detailed, giving the candidate credibility. He also gives a balanced response by explaining how the post can be improved.

When you walk down the supermarket aisle, what product jumps out and says "buy me" and why?

CHILE   AUSTRALIA   CALIFORNIA

Screenshot Delhaize

CANDIDATE: My favorite packaging comes from the wine brand, 365, which is a private label wine from Delhaize, a Belgian supermarket chain.

When I evaluate packaging, I use the "stop, hold, close" method popularized by P&G. First, does the packaging make me pause as a shopper? Then, do I take a moment to read the label? And lastly, do I put the product in the cart?

Stop

174

With 365, I stop. The wine labels are unique, cute and creative. Each wine has a decorative cork that symbolizes the wine's region: Easter Island statues for Chile, koalas for Australia and Native American Indians for California. Compare those labels with a normal wine label below, and you'll see what I mean.

Screenshot Granito

Hold

It's natural for me to inspect the wine bottle. I see that it's bargain-priced, which is consistent with 365's simple, straightforward packaging.

Close

The packaging, more so than a conventional wine, persuades me to buy. With a bargain-price, I'm willing to give it a try.

Scorecard

Overall Rating	Above Average
Marketing Aptitude	Above Average
Plan	Excellent
Communication Skills	Above Average
Composure	Excellent
Satisfying Conclusion	Above Average

Comments

Candidate chose an unforgettable example; bonus points for choosing a non-American brand. That helps the candidate standout.

The candidate's usage of P&G's "Stop, Hold, Close" framework was very clever. Not only was it appropriate, but also it showed that the candidate kept abreast of best practices in the consumer packaged goods arena.

The candidate's justifications were good, but could have used a little bit more depth.

Give me an example of an innovative product package.

CANDIDATE: Thelma's bakes and delivers warm, fresh cookies to customers. The reason it jumps out and says "buy me" because the packaging reinforces the value proposition: freshly baked cookies. The packaging also stands out from other cookie packages; the creativity piques consumer interest. (I've included a conventional cookie package example for reference.)

Screenshot / Chips Ahoy

Lastly, the packaging is functional. The cardboard material reminds me of sturdy pizza boxes, something that can withstand a harsh journey.

Scorecard

Overall Rating	Above Average
Marketing Aptitude	Above Average
Plan	Above Average
Communication Skills	Above Average
Composure	Excellent
Satisfying Conclusion	Above Average

Comments

Evaluating packaging is similar to evaluating advertising. The candidate chose a creative example, providing three reasons why the packaging is exceptional.

The response is fairly short so it may not feel convincing to the listener.

Chapter 11 Dealing with PR Disasters

What is the Interviewer Looking For?

The interviewer might ask you questions on how you might deal with a product flaw or a bad customer service interaction.

The purpose of this question is to test your communication abilities. All corporations will find themselves in a spot where they have to deal with a suboptimal situation involving a skeptical or angry audience. The interviewer wants to see if you can propose a communication plan that minimizes a negative consumer reaction.

How to Approach the Question

For most questions on handling PR disasters, I'd recommend the following PR framework:

1. Quickly apologize for the mistake
2. Contact everyone who is affected by the issue
3. Investigate what is happening
4. Implement long-term remedies
5. Communicate throughout the process

Practice Question

1. Customers claim that your drinks, which have been identified with E. coli as the reason for two infant deaths. Walk me through your PR plan for this issue.

Answer

Customers claim that your drinks, which have been identified with E. coli as the reason for two infant deaths. Walk me through your PR plan for this issue.

CANDIDATE: Give me a moment to collect my thoughts.

Candidate takes 20 seconds

CANDIDATE: I'd start by having our CEO acknowledge the situation and apologize for what happened. I'd have him fly immediately to the victim's families to provide condolences and offer to help during their grieving period.

Next, I'd ask the finance team to analyze the impact of pulling product from the shelves. Should the company pull product for the entire network or just a few geographic locations? Or would it be more prudent to just pull batches made after a certain date?

Based on the analysis, we'll make a decision to pull the product and communicate the decision to the world. At the same time, announce an investigation into the problem.

After the investigation completes, explain what happened. Determine how much should be paid to the victims and implement new processes to minimize the re-occurrence from happening. Communicate this broadly.

To summarize, I would want us to quickly acknowledge the situation, take appropriate actions and communicate our progress early and often. This will show our seriousness and sincerity in addressing the issue.

Scorecard

Overall Rating	Excellent
Marketing Aptitude	Excellent
Plan	Excellent
Communication Skills	Excellent
Composure	Excellent
Satisfying Conclusion	Excellent

Comments

The candidate shared a thoughtful approach to a PR disaster: acknowledge, apologize and take action to show seriousness and sincerity. Finally, communicate early and often to show progress, minimize confusion and effort toward making things right.

Chapter 12 Getting Analytical: Estimation

Taking a cue from management consulting firms, marketing interviewers commonly use estimation questions to gauge a candidate's analytical skills. Here are some examples:

- Estimate how many pairs of lipstick are sold each year.
- Estimate how many shoes are sold in the US each year.

Estimation questions are grounded in real world practicality. Finance, procurement and sales depend on the brand manager to produce a sales forecast.

Finance will use a sales forecast to set expectations with shareholders. Procurement will order production materials with the goal of minimizing waste. And sales will determine where to allocate their time and how many hours to invest in training based on expected customer demand.

What is the Interviewer Looking For?

For estimation questions, interviewers are assessing your listening skills and problem solving skills. They're also testing your business judgment. It wouldn't make sense if I said that only 100 pairs of lipstick have been sold in New York City, would it?

How to Approach the Question

There are two ways to answer estimation questions: top down and bottoms up.

Top Down Estimation Method

The top down approach starts with the whole and working its way down to the parts. For instance, to estimate sales of an Xbox console, a top down approach would start from the total available market — that is, anyone who can afford an Xbox. In this case, a candidate might start with the U.S. population, a little over 315 million, then hone in on the target market, which is a subset of the available market.

Bottom Up Estimation Method

The bottom up approach hinges on observations. That is, collect a single data point and then assume that what's true for a single data point can be assumed for the data point in question. For instance, if we are trying to estimate iPhone sales in the United States, we might start by visiting a single Apple store in New York City. With a clipboard in hand, we might ask outgoing customers whether they bought an iPhone. After an hour's worth of data, we can make inferences on how many iPhones are sold in the store in a given day, month or year. And from there, we can infer sales across all Apple stores in the United States.

Practice Question

1. Estimate how much it would cost for Costco to operate a drone delivery program in San Francisco.

Answer

Estimate how much it would cost for Costco to operate a drone delivery program in San Francisco.

CANDIDATE: I'll start the question by estimating the number of drones needed based on the number of Costco members in San Francisco (SF), frequency of deliveries and quantity purchased.

Then, with the number of drones, I'll estimate the cost of purchasing and operating the drones.

INTERVIEWER: I like your approach.

CANDIDATE: Let's jump in. I'll assume there are one million residents in SF. Does that work for you?

INTERVIEWER: Sure.

CANDIDATE: Fewer families live in a city, so let's assume that there are two people per household. That gives us 500,000 households in SF. Now I need to estimate the number of households with a Costco card. About 30% of my friends have a Costco card, but I don't think everyone fits into my friends middle class demographic. So I'll go with 15%, which is half that.

INTERVIEWER: Sounds good.

CANDIDATE: Now let's estimate the number of deliveries per week. Will the drone service deliver all types of goods, or only certain types?

INTERVIEWER: Costco's drone service will only deliver groceries.

CANDIDATE: Is there a weight limitation?

INTERVIEWER: Drone technology today can only deliver 5 pounds, but our scientists have created a super drone that can deliver 25 pounds.

CANDIDATE: With a drone delivery service, Costco members would be excited to order groceries weekly. Let's assume each person eats about eight pounds of Costco food each week. With two people per household, that's 16 pounds of food.

INTERVIEWER: I'm following you so far.

CANDIDATE: Do you know what percent of Costco members will take advantage of drone delivery?

INTERVIEWER: We have no idea.

CANDIDATE: Is there an additional charge for the service?

INTERVIEWER: We're planning to charge $10 for each delivery.

CANDIDATE: With a $10 delivery fee, I think many people will still find it compelling. I'll put myself out there and say there's 30% adoption rate.

INTERVIEWER: Okay.

CANDIDATE: With a 30% adoption rate, that means 22,500 deliveries per week. Can I assume that the drones take an hour per delivery and deliver 24 hours a day, 7 days a week?

INTERVIEWER: Sure.

CANDIDATE: Each drone can make 168 deliveries per week, not counting downtime or maintenance time. Divide 22,500 deliveries by 168, and we get…134 drones. Does that sound about right?

INTERVIEWER: Yes.

CANDIDATE: Now we need to estimate how much the cost of the 134 drones. Some costs that I have in mind: drones, fuel and any other administrative costs such as marketing, programming, etc. Do you have those numbers?

INTERVIEWER: Assume that each drone is the same price of a cheap car: $10,000. They are electric powered, but for now assume that it's marginal. We expect administrative costs to be an annual $50 million charge.

CANDIDATE: Multiplying and adding those numbers we get $51.38 million.

INTERVIEWER: Thanks.

Scorecard

Overall Rating	Excellent
Marketing Aptitude	Excellent
Plan	Excellent
Communication Skills	Excellent
Composure	Excellent
Satisfying Conclusion	Excellent

Comments

The candidate approached the interview with a clear plan and asked relevant questions. He also guided the interviewer through his thinking and calculations without making the interviewer feel that she's been left behind.

Chapter 13 Getting Analytical: ROI Calculations

Many marketers report campaign performance as part of their day-to-day responsibilities. To evaluate a candidate's ability to report campaign results, many hiring managers are asking candidates to calculate campaign ROI during the interview. Here are some sample questions:

- What's the ROI from the email marketing campaign?
- What's the ROI from on our search engine marketing campaign?

What is the Interviewer Looking For?

Interviewers are looking for the candidate's ability to:

- Identify vital campaign metrics
- Calculate numbers
- Explain the results, along with suitable recommendations

How to Approach the Question

For ROI questions, I'd recommend using the ROI worksheet.

ROI Worksheet

	Description	Source
Cost and Audience		
Campaign Cost	Self-explanatory (SE)	Provided
Audience Size	How many people are you reaching?	Provided
Cost per Contact	SE	Calculation
Responses		
Response Rate	How many respond to your ad?	Provided
Number of Responses	SE	Calculation

Cost per Response	SE	Calculation
Conversions		
Conversion Rate	How many customers purchase?	Provided
Number of Conversions	SE	Calculation
Cost per Conversion	SE	Calculation
Revenue		
Revenue per Conversion	How much do customers buy when they purchase?	Calculation
Total Revenue	SE	Calculation
Profit		
Profit	SE	Calculation
ROI	SE	Calculation

Marketers may want to track additional metrics based on the advertising medium. For example, in pay-per-click advertising, you'd want to track click through rates. While in email marketing, you'd want to track open rates. Add these medium-specific metrics to your ROI calculations.

Depending on the individual, some interviewers will provide the metrics indicated as "provided." However, sometimes the interviewer may ask you to make an assumption. To save you time, I've put some industry-standard assumptions that you can use at your interview.

Industry-Standard Marketing Assumptions

Metric	Industry Assumption
Online banner ad click through rate (CTR)	0.1%
Search engine marketing CTR	2%
Facebook ad CTR	0.1%
Email marketing open rate	10%
Email market CTR	5%
Direct mail response rate	4%
e-Commerce conversion rates	3%

Source: Google, Wordstream, Direct Mail Association, SilverPop

Practice Questions

1. What's the ROI on our email marketing campaign?

2. What's the ROI of our pay-per-click campaign?

3. You have an opportunity to advertise inside a New York cab. How much should you pay?

Answers

What's the ROI on our email marketing campaign?

INTERVIEWER: We recently ran an email marketing campaign. I'd like you to calculate the ROI and then tell us if we should repeat the campaign.

CANDIDATE: Here's how I would approach the question:

Candidate writes the following:

	Value	Source
Cost and Audience		
Campaign Cost		Provided
Audience Size		Provided
Cost per Contact		Calculation
Responses		
Open Rate		Provided
Click Through rate		Provided
Number of Responses		Calculation
Cost per Response		Calculation
Conversions		
Conversion Rate		Provided
Number of Conversions		Calculation
Cost per Conversion		Calculation
Revenue		
Revenue per Conversion		Provided
Total Revenue		Calculation
Profit		
Profit		Calculation
ROI		Calculation

INTERVIEWER: I like your plan. Go ahead.

CANDIDATE: Great, let's run through my checklist. How much did the campaign cost, and how many people did it reach?

INTERVIEWER: The campaign cost $5,000, and we reached 20,000 people.

CANDIDATE: What were the open rate and the click through rate?

INTERVIEWER: It was 15% and 10% respectively.

CANDIDATE: How many conversions did we get from the campaign, and how much revenue did we get from each conversion?

INTERVIEWER: Our conversion rate was 2%, and our tracked revenue was $75 per conversion.

CANDIDATE: Give me a moment to complete my calculations.

	Value	Source
Cost and Audience		
Campaign Cost	$5,000	Provided
Audience Size	20,000	Provided
Cost per Contact	$0.25	Calculation
Response Rate		
Open Rate	15%	Provided
Click Through rate	10%	Provided
Number of Responses	2,000	Calculation
Cost per Response	$2.50	Calculation
Conversions		
Conversion Rate	2%	Provided
Number of Conversions	40	Calculation
Cost per Conversion	$125	Calculation

Revenue		
Revenue per Conversion	$75	Provided
Total Revenue	$3,000	Calculation
Profit		
Profit	$-2,000	Calculation
ROI	-40%	Calculation

CANDIDATE: We lost $2,000 on the campaign, giving us a negative 40% ROI. I'd investigate whether or not we could have improved the campaign list, email message or conversion page. If not, I'd recommend that we not pursue this email marketing campaign again.

Scorecard

Overall Rating	Excellent
Marketing Aptitude	Excellent
Plan	Excellent
Communication Skills	Excellent
Composure	Excellent
Satisfying Conclusion	Excellent

Comments

Candidate efficiently asked the right questions and got to the right answer. When the numbers are available, the calculations are straightforward.

What's the ROI of our pay-per-click campaign?

INTERVIEWER: We started a pay-per-click (PPC) campaign a couple weeks ago. We'd like you to analyze the campaign ROI and recommend whether we should continue our PPC efforts.

CANDIDATE: Here's how I'd like to approach the question:

	Value	Source
Cost and Audience		
Campaign Cost		Provided
Number of Impressions		Provided
Cost per Thousand Impressions		Calculation
Response Rate		
Click Through rate		Provided
Clicks		Calculation
Cost per Click		Calculation
Conversions		
Conversion Rate		Provided
Number of Conversions		Calculation
Cost per Conversion		Calculation
Revenue		
Revenue per Conversion		Provided
Total Revenue		Calculation
Profit		
Profit		Calculation
ROI		Calculation

CANDIDATE: Does this look good to you? If so, I'd like to ask questions to fill in my checklist.

INTERVIEWER: Sure, go ahead.

CANDIDATE: How much did the campaign cost, and how many clicks did you get?

INTERVIEWER: We paid $875 for the campaign. The reports indicate that we got 20,000 impressions and a 2.5% CTR.

CANDIDATE: What was the conversion rate, and what was the tracked revenue per conversion?

INTERVIEWER: The conversion rate was 11%. We received an average of $200 per conversion.

CANDIDATE: Perfect, that's all the questions I have. Give me a moment to make some calculations.

Candidate takes 2 minutes to make calculations and fill in the table below

	Value	Source
Cost and Audience		
Campaign Cost	$875	Provided
Number of Impressions	20,000	Provided
Cost per Thousand Impressions	$43.75	Calculation
Response Rate		
Click Through rate	2.5%	Provided
Clicks	500	Calculation
Cost per Click	$1.75	Calculation
Conversions		
Conversion Rate	11%	Provided
Number of Conversions	55	Calculation
Cost per Conversion	$15.91	Calculation
Revenue		
Revenue per Conversion	$200	Provided
Total Revenue	$11,000	Calculation
Profit		
Profit	$10,125	Calculation
ROI	1157%	Calculation

CANDIDATE: Based on the provided information and my calculations, the campaign netted a profit of $10,125. That's an ROI of 1157%. Is that above your ROI target?

INTERVIEWER: Yes, we normally target a 10X return on our PPC advertising spend.

CANDIDATE: You beat that goal. Continue to run these PPC ads.

Scorecard

Overall Rating	Excellent
Marketing Aptitude	Excellent
Plan	Excellent
Communication Skills	Excellent
Composure	Excellent
Satisfying Conclusion	Excellent

Comments

This is a wonderful response. Note that the candidate asked about the company's ROI target. Most marketers have an ROI target to reflect the overall contribution they expect a campaign to provide. Many e-commerce companies use a 10X ROI as their benchmark.

You have an opportunity to advertise inside a New York cab. How much should you pay?

INTERVIEWER: A cab company gives an opportunity to promote your tour bus business to their passengers. What's the maximum you're willing to pay for this opportunity?

CANDIDATE: Here's how I'd like to approach the opportunity. First, I'd calculate the number of impressions, the conversion rate, and the expected revenue per conversion. From the revenue, we'll get a sense of the maximum we're willing to pay to breakeven.

INTERVIEWER: Sounds like a good plan.

CANDIDATE: There are a couple of questions I'd like to ask you. Where will our ad be placed?

INTERVIEWER: Your ad will be prominently placed in the back of the taxi cab. It'll be distributed in 1,000 taxi cabs.

CANDIDATE: How many passengers will see it?

INTERVIEWER: What's your best guess?

CANDIDATE: Let's say a typical taxi cab operates 6 days a week, 12 hours a day. During a 12 hour shift, let's say a driver picks up 18 fares. Let's say it is approximately two passengers per fare.

INTERVIEWER: Sounds good. What do you need to know next?

CANDIDATE: Of the passengers that sit in a cab with our advertisement, what percent will purchase a tour bus package from us?

INTERVIEWER: I'll leave that to you to estimate.

CANDIDATE: Not everyone who sits in a cab will be interested in a tour bus package. Our offering will appeal most to tourists. I'll estimate that 15 percent of all cab passengers are tourists. Of those that see our ad, I'll estimate that only one percent would be interested in our offering.

INTERVIEWER: Ok, let's go with that number.

CANDIDATE: What's the average price of a tour bus package?

INTERVIEWER: It's $30.

CANDIDATE: I have all the numbers that I need. Give me a moment to do some calculations.

Candidate makes calculations and writes the following on the whiteboard

	Value	Source
Audience		
Number of Cabs	1,000	Provided
Passengers per Cab per Week	216	Assumption & calculation
Passengers per Week	216,000	Calculation
Conversions		
Conversion Rate	1%	Assumption
Conversions per Week	2,160	Calculation
Revenue		
Revenue per Conversion	$30	Provided
Total Revenue per Week	$64,800	Calculation

CANDIDATE: Based on my calculations, we can expect $64,800 in weekly revenue from this opportunity. Do you have an ROI target for this campaign?

INTERVIEWER: We'd like to see an 800% ROI on our investments.

CANDIDATE: Ok, let me do a quick calculation to see the maximum we'd pay for this tactic.

Candidate writes the following

- ROI = (Gain from Investment – Cost of Investment) / (Cost of Investment)
- ROI * Cost of Investment = (Gain from Investment – Cost of Investment)

- ROI * Cost of Investment + Cost of Investment = Gain from Investment
- Cost of Investment * (ROI + 1) = Gain from Investment
- Cost of Investment = (Gain from Investment) / (ROI +1)
- Cost of Investment = $64,800 / (800% + 1)
- Cost of Investment = $7,200

CANDIDATE: Based on my calculations, we should pay no more than $7,200 for the opportunity.

Scorecard

Overall Rating	Excellent
Marketing Aptitude	Excellent
Plan	Excellent
Communication Skills	Excellent
Composure	Excellent
Satisfying Conclusion	Excellent

Comments

The candidate deftly used the ROI worksheet to work his way toward a maximum campaign cost he'd be willing to pay.

This wasn't an easy question. A lot of math was involved; the candidate gets a lot of credit for being patient and maintaining his composure. Well done.

Chapter 14 Strategizing: CEO-level Issues

What is the Interviewer Looking For?

With CEO-level issues, the interviewer is trying to understand your ability to think strategically about the business. That is, can you filter out critical issues from less urgent ones? Do you know how the company makes money and the levers that impact its business model? Do you know which trends represent the biggest threats and why?

How to Approach the Question

Strategy questions on CEO-level issues usually relate to competitive or operational issues.

No need to memorize new frameworks. Simply think about the critical drivers for operational or competitive issue. Take a stance and discuss the pros and cons of what's been analyzed or proposed.

Practice Questions

1. What brand is not doing well, and why?
2. Should Starbucks have an express line?

Answers

What brand is not doing well, and why?

CANDIDATE: Give me a moment to collect my thoughts.

Candidate pauses for 30 seconds

CANDIDATE: Let me ask you, what's your favorite online travel agency (OTA)?

Expedia.

CANDIDATE: Name another.

Kayak.

CANDIDATE: And another.

Hipmunk.

CANDIDATE: The company I'm thinking of is Orbitz. If you're a travel agency and a typical consumer can't name your company, there's a problem.

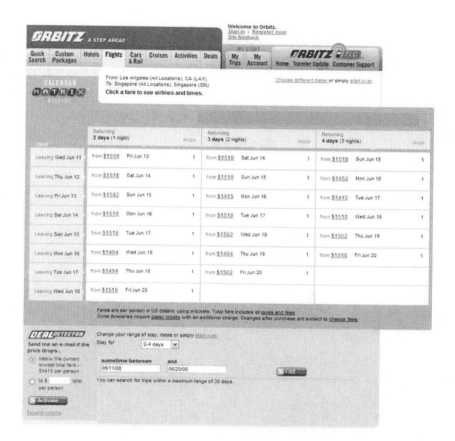

CANDIDATE: The reason I believe you did not name Orbitz is that they don't have a unique brand identity. For example, when you think of Priceline, you think of bidding for travel and William Shatner, their spokesperson. When you think of Hotels.com, you immediately think of Hotels.com as a destination for booking hotels, not airline tickets or rental cars.

The second problem: Orbitz is not wisely spending its marketing dollars. I compared Orbitz's financials with Priceline's, the industry leader:

	Orbitz	Priceline

Marketing Expense	$253 million	$196 million
Revenue	$779 million	$5.3 billion
Return on marketing dollars	208%	2604%

Lastly, there's a worrisome trend that's affecting the broader online travel agencies, including Orbitz: Consumers are getting more comfortable finding the best prices using non-OTAs such as Google and Bing. Consumers also prefer booking directly from the airlines and hotels for the following reasons:

1. They feel airlines and hotels provide second-rate service to customers who book through travel agencies.

2. When a problem arises, many customers don't want to deal with a travel agency, who serves as a needless intermediary between customer and the travel vendor, whether it's a hotel, airline, or rental car agency.

One more thing: it's never good when your brand gets confused with another.

Murphy USA: Coupon for a Free Pack of Orbitz Gum
Published: Thursday, March 15, 2012, 12:15 PM

By Christie Dedman -- The Birmingham News
Follow

Recommend   Be the first of your friends to recommend this.

Comment   0   Share
Tweet   0   Email
g+1   0   Print

Go here to register with Murphy USA stores and get a coupon for a free pack of Orbitz gum.

You can sign in or create an account and you should see the coupon good through March 21.

Screenshot / Birmingham Bargain Mom

Scorecard

Overall Rating	Above Average
Marketing Aptitude	Above Average
Plan	Above Average
Communication Skills	Above Average
Composure	Above Average
Satisfying Conclusion	Above Average

Comments

The opening theatric was interesting and created mystique. This is overall a solid discussion with key evidence showing why the Orbitz brand is weak and needs help.

Should Starbucks have an express line?

INTERVIEWER: You are a marketing manager focused on the Starbucks retail experience. Our customer feedback portal, My Starbucks Idea, indicates that quick ordering is important to customers. A large minority has requested an express line for simple orders such as drip coffee or a pastry.

What are the pros and cons of implementing an express line, and what would you recommend?

CANDIDATE: Give me a moment to collect my thoughts.

INTERVIEWER: Sure.

Candidate takes 30 seconds

CANDIDATE: Here are some pros and cons when it comes to having an express line:

Pros

- Shorter wait time for simple orders
- Process more customers in a single store, increasing store revenue
- Shorter lines give customers the impression that orders will be fulfilled more quickly

Cons

- Shorter wait time reduces likelihood customer will make an impulse purchase
- Two separate lines could create confusion
- A single line allows baristas to help out on a variety of orders, improving productivity
- Some Starbucks stores are so small they cannot accommodate room for a second line
- Extra Starbucks baristas would be necessary for a second line, increasing costs
- Having a single dedicated simple order line can create monotony for baristas, reducing job satisfaction
- Having a speedy checkout line minimizes the opportunity for baristas to connect with customers; this runs counter to Starbucks' emphasis on customer experience

This is a hard call. There are good reasons for and against an express line. At the end of the day, I'd recommend that we experiment and see what happens with an express line. So I'd order up a pilot test with a few Starbucks stores, collect data and reassess before making a broader recommendation.

Scorecard

Overall Rating	Excellent
Marketing Aptitude	Excellent
Plan	Excellent
Communication Skills	Excellent
Composure	Excellent
Satisfying Conclusion	Excellent

Comments

Candidate brilliantly brainstormed a long and thoughtful list of potential reasons for and against an express line. The candidate was caught in a difficult position to make a recommendation when the list indicated no clear winner. He made the correct decision to recommend a pilot test.

Chapter 15 Answering Off-The-Wall Questions

Sometimes candidates are given off-the-wall interview questions that appear to have no relation with the position you're interviewing for. For instance:

- Who's your favorite musician?
- If you could be any superhero, who would it be?
- Which historical figures would you invite to dinner and why?

What Is the Interviewer Looking For?

Most interviewers would explain that they ask these questions to assess a candidate's ability to think quickly, showcase their personality and demonstrate creativity. A small handful might admit that they ask off-the-wall questions to lighten up the interview.

So make it fun and make it creative. Present a dull and formal response at your own risk!

How to Approach the Question

Treat this question as a personal brand question. That is, what would you like to be known for? Perhaps you want to be known as someone who is a quiet leader that adapts to change. In this case, your favorite superhero might be Wolverine, a superhero who exemplifies quiet leadership and ability to adapt to many situations.

How do you determine your personal brand? You'll find your personal brand intersecting between where your strengths lie and what the employer is looking for in an ideal candidate. The last part is critical. Your employer has a picture in their mind of what skills and traits the ideal candidate has. To increase your chances of getting the job, synchronize your response to this question with what they're looking for.

One last tip, despite the seemingly inconsequential nature of off-the-wall interview questions, you are still being judged, so take the question seriously.

Practice Questions

1.   What animal would you be?
2.   What would the title of your autobiography be?

Answers

What animal would you be?

CANDIDATE: Huh?

INTERVIEWER: That's my question: what animal would you be?

CANDIDATE: Are you serious?

INTERVIEWER: Yes, I want you to answer that question.

CANDIDATE: Okay, let me think about it.

Candidate pauses for 15 seconds

CANDIDATE: I guess it would be a giraffe.

INTERVIEWER: And why is that?

CANDIDATE: Well because I have a long neck. And I walk slowly.

Scorecard

Overall Rating	Poor
Marketing Aptitude	Poor
Plan	Poor
Communication Skills	Poor
Composure	Poor
Satisfying Conclusion	Poor

Comments

This response is problematic for many reasons. First, the candidate skeptical tone could be construed as being disrespectful. Second, the candidate's explanation for why he chose giraffe was disappointing because it was too literal. It doesn't give showcase the candidate's creativity or personality.

A much better explanation might be: "I choose giraffe. The reason I choose giraffe is because my co-workers have always told me that my decision-making capabilities are similar to President Obama. That is, I survey the landscape and look at the data. When I make a decision, I am very deliberate and move decisively. When I think of animals that are known for surveying the situation and deliberate in their actions, giraffe was the first one that came to mind."

What would the title of your autobiography be?

CANDIDATE: I've never thought about writing an autobiography, so you've stumped me. But let me give it some thought.

Candidate takes 20 seconds

CANDIDATE: I'd call the title of my autobiography, *Stein Stung by the Sea.*

INTERVIEWER: Why did you choose that?

CANDIDATE: There are a couple reasons. First, Stein refers to my last name. Second, I've always loved the water. I remember my childhood days in Cape Cod where I sit on the porch with my grandfather or go beachcombing with my sister. Third, I chose the word "stung" because my nickname growing up was Buzz. It was partly because of my buzz cut, but others said it was my social skills, exhibited by my different groups of friends and wild stories. Lastly, I just kind of like the alliteration. It rolls right off the tongue.

Scorecard

Overall Rating	Excellent
Marketing Aptitude	Excellent
Plan	Excellent
Communication Skills	Excellent
Composure	Excellent
Satisfying Conclusion	Excellent

Comments

The candidate handled the question gracefully. It was an odd question, but he was up for the challenge. He came up with a unique and memorable title, full of thoughtful significance. We also learned quite a bit about the candidate: his Cape Cod childhood, buzz cut and about his social skills.

Chapter 16 Answering Behavioral Interview Questions

One of my colleagues called behavioral interviews the free throw of interview questions. It's an apt description. On the one hand, behavioral interviews seem like a breeze relative to these difficult case questions. On the other hand, just like in basketball, outcomes can be won or lost by a few missed free throws. In other words, don't take the behavioral section of the interview too lightly.

Behavioral interviews are questions about your past experiences. They typically begin with either "Tell me a time…" or "Give me an example…"

Common Behavioral Interview Questions at the Marketing Interview

Tell me a time when you…

- Improved sales or market share with a marketing campaign.
- Persuaded someone to your point of view.
- Communicated a difficult topic.
- Were asked to do something you didn't think was right.
- Developed an innovative solution to a problem.
- Analyzed or interpreted numerical or financial information.
- Led a team.
- Dealt with a difficult team member.
- Intervened to get your team back on track because they couldn't resolve or decide on an issue.
- Made the biggest mistake in your career.

The behavioral questions can range from leadership to influencing others to end-to-end marketing experience.

Why Behavioral Interviews Are Becoming More Popular

In 2013, Google's HR department found that behavioral interviews are the best predictors of employee success. For instance, if they asked you, "Tell me a time when you improved sales with a marketing campaign," the hiring manager would know that if you were presented with a similar situation in the future, you would perform similarly, if not better.

What Is the Interviewer Looking For?

For an ideal response, interviewers are looking for two things: credibility and likability.

For credibility, they're assessing whether you have the competence to do the job. Here are some factors they want to see in your response:

- **Owner vs. participant**. In today's cross-functional organizations, many interview candidates claimed they led a big project or delivered big results. However, if you dig a bit deeper, you'll find the candidate played a marginal role. Or the candidate may have participated in portions of the project, not the entire thing. To uncover the truth, savvy interviewers will ask follow-up questions including who was involved, what you personally did and how you did it. It may feel uncomfortable to receive 20 questions on a particular experience, but I have found that it is to your benefit to play along. It will more quickly answer the doubts that percolate in the interviewer's mind.

- **Great versus "just good" achievement**. Interview candidates are clever. They realize that including numbers into their resumes and interview responses sound more impressive. But even savvier interviewers will want to determine why it was considered a great versus "just good" achievement. And they want to know whether the results were largely due to your impact, or if those results would have occurred even without your involvement. Expect the interviewer ask follow up questions on baseline metrics such as "How much growth did you see last year?" or "What was the projected increase had you decided not to invest in a new feature?"

We've established your talent by choosing and delivering stories that demonstrate your exceptional experiences, skills and impact. But likability is the other critical piece to the behavioral interview. It's equally important to develop chemistry or rapport with the interviewer.

Interviewers like to advocate candidates that remind them of themselves. They see themselves as talented and entertaining. For interviewers who potentially meet multiple candidates a week, nothing can be more tedious than a candidate who can't find a punch line in their responses or talk about their past experiences with the same excitement as watching paint dry.

Not every candidate is a comedian, so I'm not going to press or even encourage you to tell a joke if that doesn't come naturally to you. But you do have to be entertaining and more importantly, earn the listener's full attention.

Your goal is to tell stories in a way that has the listener on the edge of their seat, eager to hear more. To achieve this goal, shift your mindset. Tell your stories like a world-class storyteller. Think of your favorite storyteller. It could be J.K. Rowling, Stephen King, or Steven Spielberg. Thinking through the basics of a satisfying story, there are three key elements:

- **Colorful characters and settings**. Be specific. People (and places) have names. Characters have motivations, perspectives and emotions. You're at the center of the story, so you'll be the hero. And every hero has a villain. To summarize, don't forget the who, what, why, how and when of what you're describing.

- **Conflict**. Every good story has conflict that needs to be resolved. For instance, Superman can choose to save five million people in New York City from a flaming meteor or his girlfriend, Lois Lane, in Des Moines, Iowa. Life is about dilemmas, tradeoffs and tough decisions. Good conflicts include unreasonable constraints, impossible deadlines and Earth-shattering consequences.

- **Resolution.** Every story should have an ending. That is, it has to have a satisfying end where the conflict ends. More often than not, the hero wins. But other times, the hero doesn't win. In those circumstances, there are valuable lessons from a loss that needs to be articulated to the listener.

Just because you're discussing a career experience, it doesn't mean you have to recount your career with the same humdrum delivery as a corporate status meeting.

One more tip: Every story has a natural progression that covers the beginning, middle and end. Don't leave the listener wondering: how did it all start? Or make the interviewer think: did you defeat your foe eventually?

How to Approach the Question

I do not advocate the STAR (situation, task, action and result) interviewing method. It's so poorly practiced by interview candidates everywhere that it's become synonymous with lifeless, robotic delivery. I've developed my own framework, which more naturally directs the candidate toward the storytelling principles discussed previously. The framework is called the DIGS method™. The phrase "Can you dig it?" has two meanings. First, do you understand? Second, are you enjoying the moment? We want interview stories that hiring managers understand and enjoy. Hence, the DIGS method™:

D ramatize the situation
I ndicate the alternatives
G o through what you did
S ummarize your impact

I've refined the DIGS method™ with hundreds of clients. I've always thought that the best way to interview is to pretend that the interview is a casual conversation between two friends. The DIGS method™ will get your there.

What is the DIGS method™?
Dramatize the situation

Imagine this fictional conversation with the CEO of a Fortune 500 retailer:

ME: What did you do today?

CEO: I wrote some emails. I went some meetings. And I yelled at some people.

ME: Oh, guess what, I did same exact thing. Emails, meetings and yelled at people. I guess I can do your job.

CEO: No, no, no. You don't get it. When I was writing some emails, I wrote to John Doe, our chief legal counsel. John is trying to fight a $2 billion dollar, anti-trust fine from the European Union. When I was meeting with someone, I was meeting with Jane Doe, manufacturer of this year's hottest toy, to discuss whether the manufacturer should *allocate $20 million dollars of inventory to our retail company. When I yelled at some people...*

ME: *Ah, I guess I can't do your job.*

The key takeaway: context and details matter. If we reduce our jobs to the core elements, it's mundane and unremarkable. Dramatize the situation and help us understand why your job, project, or product is important.

Indicate the alternatives

This is an optional step, but if you can do it, you'll be a rock star. When I think about behavioral interviews, it's about problem solving. You're solving problems with people, products, processes, etc.

Any good problem solver knows that there's more than one way to solve a problem. So why not describe all the alternative solutions?

Without the alternatives, the listener just might think to him or herself: "What's so special about that? I would have done it the same exact way." Candidates can't settle for being normal. This is the interview. Candidates need to stand out from others. They need to be special.

The use of alternatives uses the same theatrical device as dramatizing the situation: it helps us appreciate why what you did was so important.

In general, you'd want to list three different alternatives. One alternative is not enough. Two is better. Three feels complete. But more than three is not necessary; the listener will feel overwhelmed.

Lastly, talk about the pros and cons of each of the three approaches. You'll be perceived as thoughtful and analytical, which traits they'll look for in top product managers.

Go through what you did

Drop us off on the front lines of action. Give us the details of what you did. Who did you call? What did you ask them to do? How did they respond? What kind of resistance did you get?

By putting the listener in your shoes, you convince us that you were the front-line owner and driving, not a participant who was lingering in the back-row, several steps removed from the core action and the results.

Summarize the impact

Conclude your story by summarizing the impact. Without a summary, you'll leave the listener with the *So What?* feeling. Show the listener that your actions benefited the business' bottom line.

Clean, crisp numbers make a big impact. Did your project reduce costs by 5 percent or increase revenue by $100 million? Yes, those numbers are hard to recall. I barely remember what happened last week. But if you don't remember if the revenue increase was $1 or $100 million, estimate the impact, if you must.

If there are instances where you've racked your brain and can't come up with a reasonable (estimated) number, a qualitative statement could work too. It could be a quote from a senior executive who thought you executed the smoothest product launch that he's seen in last five years. It could be a testimonial from a retailer who said you handled a product recall with poise.

Either way, a qualitative statement that validates your impact can be just as good.

Practice Questions

1. Tell me a time when you received criticism. What was it, and how do you respond?

2. Tell me a time when you had to communicate a difficult business decision.

3. Give me an example of a situation where you had to overcome major obstacles to achieve your objectives.

Answers

Tell me a time when you received criticism. What was it, and how do you respond?

CANDIDATE: Eighteen months ago, I sat down with my boss, Bryan, the division VP. He said, "Clint, I had a meeting with Kelly on your team. She told me that you've been ineffective in running your staff meetings. I'd like you to address it."

My blood boiled. First, I couldn't believe that my boss went around me and solicited input from my direct reports. Second, I didn't understand why my own direct report would not tell something to me directly. And third, I disagreed with the feedback. No one ever told me that my meeting style was a problem.

I let my emotions pass and told Bryan that I would take care of it. I attended my weekly breakfast meeting with local executives and raised the issue. My peers gave me some good suggestions. One executive emailed me the issue tracker template he used for his staff meetings. Another executive proposed that I color code issues red, yellow and green to indicate priorities.

I also solicited input from my team about how we could better run meetings. Kelly suggested that I submit a meeting agenda in advance, while another team member recommended that meeting notes be sent out after the meeting. As a written record, it would help us track key discussions and decisions. It would also help those who could not make the meeting from feeling left out.

I gave all the suggestions a shot. It was weird to try these different things. But I did get good feedback from my staff that I was responding to their input.

During my last performance review with my boss, about six months after Bryan raised the issue, he highlighted that I was "very coachable," and he specifically used this instance as an example.

Scorecard

Overall Rating	Excellent
Marketing Aptitude	Excellent
Plan	Excellent
Communication Skills	Excellent
Composure	Excellent
Satisfying Conclusion	Excellent

Comments

Candidate nailed it. He told us why he was upset by the criticism, took responsibility for the issue and resolved it with a happy ending.

Tell me a time when you had to communicate a difficult business decision.

CANDIDATE: Two years ago, I was the head of public affairs for Java Coffee Works, a global coffee company with over 20,000 stores in 45 countries. As the head of public affairs, I led a team that constantly monitored customer and employee issues, especially ones that could have an imminent negative public relations impact.

An issue that keeps coming up: Java's gun policy. We've had families confront customers that carry unconcealed firearms. And we've had baristas feel threatened when a customer complains about their Constitutional rights.

It's also a very emotional issue internally. Just 11 months before, one of our baristas was a victim in the Springtown shooting.

220

Lastly, gun rights groups have also misleadingly scheduled media events during our "Java Appreciation Days" store events, implying that Java is pro-gun rights. Our team agreed that we had to be proactive. A response would be timely, minimize confusion and increase customer and employee satisfaction.

Our CEO made it clear. We didn't want to have guns in our stores. But the stats made it clear that it would not be easy to take a stand:

- 40 percent of all Americans own guns
- 54 percent oppose stricter gun laws
- 89 percent opposed a complete gun ban.

Our first option, declaring an official policy to ban guns from all Java stores would be a polarizing PR situation. It was also likely that it would be bad for business. Images of protests and empty Starbucks counters danced in our heads.

The second option was an open letter approach. Our CEO would pen a public letter requesting that customers leave guns at home. On the one hand, it would be a request, not an official rule. It wouldn't violate Constitutional laws or infringe on anybody's rights. Customers could still bring guns to the store, but Java would make it clear that it wasn't what we preferred. On the other hand, we were worried that it might alienate our customers, depressing sales.

We went with the second approach. My team got to work and decided on four big deliverables:

1. Reach out to the field leadership, alerting them of the upcoming announcement.
2. Communicate with our front-line baristas. We explained the policy and why it was necessary. We provided a list of

frequently asked questions and tips on how to tell a conversational story around the decision.

3. Pen the CEO's letter.
4. Work with media outlets on the announcement

On announcement day, as expected, we made headlines on every major media outlet. No other nationwide retailer made such a strong stance on guns. We received tons of comments on our social media sites. Some were crass and negative, but many were supportive.

From the beginning, our success metrics revolved around:

- *Message clarity*. How many people had questions about the policy?
- *Efficiency*. How many questions did our Java leadership team receive from employees and customers about the new policy?
- *Employee satisfaction*. How many people were proud to work with Java?
- *Customer satisfaction*. How many people would continue to be Java customers?

Weeks after the announcement, we collected feedback and survey results. The announcement was received very well. Customers felt that we were clear about what we were communicating. Our leadership team received few questions about the policy, allowing them to get back to business. Most of our customers indicated that they would not boycott Java. And lastly, our employees were proud that we took a stand for their personal safety.

Scorecard

Overall Rating	Excellent
Marketing Aptitude	Excellent
Plan	Excellent

Communication Skills	Excellent
Composure	Excellent
Satisfying Conclusion	Excellent

Comments

This is as good as it gets when it comes to behavioral interview responses. The candidate communicated a complex situation with clarity and poise. And the happy ending helps!

Inspired by: http://bit.ly/SBUXGun

Give me an example of a situation where you had to overcome major obstacles to achieve your objectives.

CANDIDATE: Last May, my mom lost her job, and we couldn't pay the bills. My mom asked me to step up and take some jobs. I ended up finding two jobs, working 45 hours a week. To carve out the extra hours from my week, I had to give up my extracurricular organizations, cut back on sleep and give up my friends.

The hardest part was dealing with my friends' guilt tripping. My friends claimed that I was boring and acted like an adult. It was hard to not take it personally. I blamed my mom for ruining my social life, and I yelled at her more often than I liked.

It took a long time, but eventually I accepted my role. My mom spent years taking responsibility for me, and it was a chance for me to return the favor and take care of my mom and family.

After working the two jobs for six months, my mom finally found a job. I returned to my social life and picked up my extracurricular activities again. And I'm proud to say that during that intense time period, I maintained a B+ average in school.

Scorecard

Overall Rating	Excellent
Marketing Aptitude	Excellent
Plan	Excellent
Communication Skills	Excellent
Composure	Excellent
Satisfying Conclusion	Excellent

Comments

The narrative flows smoothly. The example demonstrates the candidate's teamwork and maturity, accepting her role and stepping up to help the family. The ending shows that while she had to make some tradeoffs, she succeeded in her dual responsibilities at school and family.

The narrative is not as detailed as the previous behavioral interview answers. But this response is from a soon-to-be college grad. Given his age, he showed remarkable awareness and maturity.

Chapter 17 Rising Above the Noise

A book named, *Rise Above the Noise*, should at least have one section about distinguishing yourself from other candidates, no? After thinking about how you can help develop marketing campaigns, we'll want to apply those same principles toward how you can market the most important product: yourself.

Develop Your Personal Brand

Develop your personal positioning statement, or brand, for each position you want to interview. What do you want to be known for? Is it your 30 years of experience? Or is it your aptitude with digital media? Whatever it is, make it clear early, often and provide evidence that lets the listener believe your claim.

When picking a personal brand, emphasize a position that's in-line with what the employer is looking for. If your potential employer looking for someone with experience with new media, it wouldn't make sense for you to emphasize only your traditional media experience would it?

Increase Awareness

Applying for a job via a corporate website is one of the least effective ways of getting your resume in front of the recruiter or hiring manager. With the Internet, most positions are bombarded with hundreds and perhaps thousands of submissions. Recruiters and hiring managers don't have time to effectively sift through submissions from the Internet.

What's a good way to have your resume float to the top? Send your resume and cover letter directly to the hiring manager. Hiring manager will never resist a relevant resume in their email inbox. After all, they are short staffed, aren't they? The sooner they can hire the ideal candidate (you), the sooner they can resume a normal work-life balance.

I wouldn't recommend sending unsolicited resumes and cover letters. It might feel a bit like spam. Instead, find an internal contact that knows the hiring manager well and would be willing to put in a good word for you. A dash of trust and a sprinkle of endorsement will likely win you a phone screen.

Stir Interest in Your Candidacy

Get hiring managers interested in your candidacy. The most traditional method is to have an informational interview with the hiring manager. But if you can't, you can easily stir interest without meeting the hiring manager face-to-face. Here are some ideas:

- Send relevant articles
- Do relevant competitive research
- Share ideas on a competitive response
- Find people to sing your praises

If you want to push the creative envelope, you can also attempt what many jobseekers have attempted from time-to-time: post your job hunt request on a billboard. Here's a recent one: the billboard showed a picture of a man in a Santa Claus hat. The text started with, "Trilingual operations manager seeks position in hotels, restaurants, tourism and leisure." And it ended with, "All I want for Christmas is a job."

I'm not suggesting that you literally try this tactic. But there is a good takeaway here: most candidates don't have the creativity, confidence and follow-through to undertake any of the activities above. Those who do, stand out.

Provide a Free Trial

Sometimes the best way to get the job is to do the job. And when you're working for free, you don't need anyone's permission.

How can you demonstrate you can do the job? Here are some ideas:

- Run a consumer survey
- Mock-up a new brochure
- Create wireframes for a new marketing website

Share your work at the beginning of the interview. If they take the bait, you'll spend the remaining interview time talking about your work. Think how big of an advantage that is. You can choose to spend your interview talking about an unanticipated question. Or you could discuss the consumer survey that you collected, analyzed and developed recommendations for over the past weekend. I'd choose the latter any day.

If they choose not to talk about the project, that's alright. Just leave your materials with the interviewer. More often than not, that physical leave behind is a reminder that you cared enough about the job that you put more time thinking about the role than any other candidate. It's not a substitute for doing well for the interview, but it does help you rise above the rest. And who knows, even if you don't review it at the interview, they might flip through your work during their next meeting or when they discuss your candidacy with the rest of the hiring team.

Don't Forget the Thank You Note

Always send a thank you note. Some interviewers care, and some don't. Don't guess which one they might be. Just do it. It creates a positive impression that makes a difference.

What's Next

Thanks for reading! However, our journey doesn't end here. First and foremost, I'd love to hear from you. Please send questions, comments, typos and edits to: lewis@impactinterview.com.

Second, I have two additional resources for you:

- Visit my website, lewis-lin.com. You'll find more resources to help you prepare for the marketing interview, including my popular cheat sheet on *How to Critique Super Bowl Ads.*
- Sign-up for my newsletter. I send articles, interview tips and new sample answers that you'll find helpful in your marketing interviews. Sign-up at lewis-lin.com.
- Find a practice partner for marketing case interviews at http://bit.ly/InterviewPartner. If marketing case interviews don't come naturally to you, the most effective way to nail them is practice!

Finally, **I have a favor to ask you. Please take a moment to review my book on Amazon:** http://amzn.to/1dM7kce. Whether you loved or hated the book, you can help me improve subsequent editions of *Rise Above the Noise* by writing a Amazon review.

Book reviews also play an important in promoting my book to a larger audience, which will turn give me a bigger opportunity to create better marketing interview preparation materials for you in the future.

Thank you for reading and reviewing *Rise Above the Noise*. May your get the marketing job of your dreams!

Lewis C. Lin

Acknowledgments

A big thank you goes to everyone involved in the book. I couldn't have done this without your feedback, thoughts and ongoing brainstorming. If I left out any of you, I apologize for the inadvertent exclusion.

Special thanks to my book cover illustrator and designer, Jenny Chui, who put together a book cover that I never would have dreamed of.

Christine Ying

Dan Frechtling

David Youn

Deny Khoung

Doug Gradt

Hugh Taylor

Jamie Hui

Jason Jennings

Luanne Calvert

Mark McLaren

Philipp von Holtzendorff-Fehling

Sabra Goldick

Sanjay Puri

Scott Shrum

Wendy White

Appendix

Additional Readings
Marketing

The 22 Immutable Laws of Branding

By Al and Laura Ries

This father and daughter tandem outlines their 22 laws on how to create a dominant brand. The authors firmly believe that key to branding success is to be the market leader and that firms should do whatever it takes to be first, biggest and best. They point out that many organizations unnecessarily extend their brands into new categories where they have weak competitive position. It's filled with copious examples that validate their concepts. It's light reading that makes you think twice about the popular brands that exist today.

Marketing Management

By Philip Kotler and Kevin Keller

This is the legendary reference book for all things marketing. There's nothing that isn't covered in this 816-page book.

Marketing Management: The Big Picture

By Christie L. Nordhielm

I'm a big fan of Nordhielm's Big Picture framework. I cover it in detail in this book, but if you'd like to go straight to the source, I'd highly recommend Nordhielm's tome.

Positioning: The Battle for Your Mind

By Al Ries, Jack Trout

230

This easy-to-read book discusses the importance of having clear product positioning.

Clay Christensen's Milkshake Marketing

By Carmen Nobel

The senior editor of HBS Working Knowledge summarizes Christensen's job-based segmentation. Christensen's philosophy is that companies should segment their markets based on "jobs-to-be-done," which is different from traditional demographic or product-based segmentation. Christensen is an HBS professor who wrote the business classic, *The Innovator's Dilemma*.

http://hbswk.hbs.edu/item/6496.html

Business History

Rising Tide: Lessons from 165 Years of Brand Building at Procter & Gamble

By Davis Dyer, Frederick Dalzell and Rowena Olegario

The authors review the evolution of Procter & Gamble, offering a historical look on how its popular brands came to be and insights on the company's marketing savvy.

Career Paths at Consumer Goods Companies

Marketing Coordinator → Assistant Brand Manager → Brand Manager → Marketing Director

Marketing Coordinator

Marketing coordinator is an entry level role for new college graduates. Key responsibilities for the marketing coordinator include:

- Business analysis and reporting
- Competitive analysis
- Executing marketing plans
- Managing marketing budgets
- Assisting with advertising copy
- Learning the business

Marketing coordinators report to the brand manager; they typically spend one to two years in the role.

Depending on the company, marketing coordinators are also known as marketing assistants, marketing associates or marketing analysts.

Assistant Brand Manager

When promoted, marketing coordinators typically become assistant brand managers. New MBA graduates also join consumer packaged goods companies at the assistant brand manager level.

At an assistant brand manager, the individual's emphasis begins to shift from execution to leadership roles. Typical responsibilities include:

- Lead teams across various functional departments on day-to-day issues
- Create marketing plans based on brand objectives and current business performance

- Develop volume and profit forecasts
- Present work to senior executives
- Mentor marketing coordinators and other junior staff
- Represent the company at various functions such as college recruiting and community outreach

Assistant brand managers report to the brand manager; they typically spend two to four years in the role.

Some companies call this role associate brand manager.

Brand Manager

An assistant brand manager, when promoted, becomes a brand manager. A brand manager is responsible for the business results of either a single major brand or a handful of smaller brands. Brand managers start to assert themselves as a senior leader on the team.

Responsibilities include:

- Manage marketing coordinators and assistant brand managers
- Be responsible for direct reports' professional development
- Develop brand strategy with the marketing director
- Take on a senior leadership role for cross-functional teams
- Participate in steering committees and policy review boards

Depending on the individual and company, brand managers typically spend two to five years in this role.

Marketing Director

A marketing director is responsible for an entire business unit. They will demonstrate leadership not only within the company, but also outside of the company as well. Expect marketing directors to represent the firm at conferences such as the American Marketing Association.

Responsibilities include:

- Develop strategy for the entire business unit
- Allocate and monitor budgets
- Manage a team of brand managers
- Determine brand goals

Some companies call marketing directors category managers or group directors.

Vice President

A vice president is responsible for an entire business division. Vice presidents are senior veterans with more than 15 years of experience. They're often tapped to lead challenging strategic projects such as new market opportunities or organizational change initiatives.

Responsibilities include:

- Monitor and strategize business performance for entire business division
- Specify division-wide budgets
- Determine annual and long-term division goals
- Manage a team of marketing directors
- Lead strategic change initiatives

Made in the USA
Lexington, KY
23 June 2018